RETIREMENT HELD HOSTAGE

How To
Rescue Your Retirement
From Bad Advice

RETIREMENT HELD HOSTAGE

How To
Rescue Your Retirement
From Bad Advice

ROBERT RUSSELL

Advantage®

Published by Advantage, Charleston, South Carolina.
Member of Advantage Media Group.

ADVANTAGE is a registered trademark and the Advantage colophon is a trademark of Advantage Media Group, Inc.

Printed in the United States of America.

ISBN: 978-159932-361-9
LCCN: 2012945044

This publication is designed to provide accurate and authoritative information in regard to the subject matter covered. It is sold with the understanding that the publisher is not engaged in rendering legal, accounting, or other professional services. If legal advice or other expert assistance is required, the services of a competent professional person should be sought.

Advantage Media Group is proud to be a part of the Tree Neutral® program. Tree Neutral offsets the number of trees consumed in the production and printing of this book by taking proactive steps such as planting trees in direct proportion to the number of trees used to print books. To learn more about Tree Neutral, please visit **www.treeneutral.com**. To learn more about Advantage's commitment to being a responsible steward of the environment, please visit **www.advantagefamily.com/green**

Advantage Media Group is a leading publisher of business, motivation, and self-help authors. Do you have a manuscript or book idea that you would like to have considered for publication? Please visit **www.advantagefamily.com** or call **1.866.775.1696**

DEDICATION

To my wife Michelle, for being my biggest fan and providing me with rock-solid support.

To my dad, for giving me the opportunity and direction to positively impact many lives. Thanks for believing in me.

To my mom and Sonny, for raising me with razor-sharp determination and a die-hard work ethic.

To my Lord, for your sacrifice and for giving me a passionate life.

ABOUT THE AUTHOR

Rob Russell's specialized advice is valued by *The Wall Street Journal*, FOX News and *U.S. News & World Report*, but he is NOT from Wall Street royalty. He is not part of the system.

With a heart of a skeptic, Rob set out to uncover ways to create and preserve wealth in both good and bad markets – ways that didn't involve the failed strategies of "buy and hope," mutual funds, or divining the actions of the U.S. government and Federal Reserve.

In this book he helps you unshackle and unleash the true potential of your retirement and put you squarely back in control of your financial future. Within these pages he shares easy-to-understand strategies that have propelled him and his company into the national limelight.

Mr. Russell is CEO/CIO of Russell & Company and works with conservative, "self-made" clients throughout the United States and abroad. Rob is a life-long resident of Ohio, where he lives with his wife and children.

He hosts a radio show, "Retirement Rescue Radio," every week on News Talk Radio WHIO and writes the "Smarter Investor" column for *U.S. News & World Report*.

Rob enjoys traveling, cooking, playing soccer and creating memorable moments with his family.

FOREWORD

You are holding this book in your hands because you have concerns about your retirement or want to confirm you are on the right track. This is a valid pursuit on your part, as we are among the first generation of people in modern history here in America who will likely be totally responsible for our own retirement.

The days of fixed lifetime pensions are almost gone. The government's ability to provide a reliable retirement is questionable at best. And your family members may be in worse shape than you are. Having your destiny in your own hands may feel scary, given economic and world conditions, but in reality, being in your own pilot's seat is the safest place to be.

Retirement has always put me in mind of a children's teeter-totter in a park or school yard. One side starts on the ground and rises until it reaches its zenith, when the other side touches the ground and starts upward. When you begin your work life, your retirement funds are at ground level, but through your working years, they move upward until, hopefully, they reach their high point at the moment you choose to retire. Then they will support you through the ride safely back to the ground.

If you remember playing on a teeter-totter, you know that you want someone reliable and dependable on the other end, because if they jump off, bounce around, or slide forward, you can be in for an uncomfortable ride or plummet to the ground.

Retirement is not an age; it is an amount of money. I have seen recent reports that tell us fully 85% of Americans do not enjoy or receive fulfillment from their jobs. This is sad in and of itself. If you are one of these unfortunate individuals, commit now to make career changes as soon as it is practical.

I was talking with a frustrated individual recently who told me he only had seven-and-a-half years to go. Not understanding what he was saying, I asked, "Seven-and-a-half years until what?" He explained that he only had seven-and-a-half years of his miserable, disgusting job until he could retire. This is one of the saddest scenarios I can imagine.

In the news not so long ago there was a report about an individual who committed a homicide and only received a sentence of six years. Staying in a "miserable and disgusting" job for one day is too much. On the other hand, if – like me – you are one of the fortunate individuals who receives satisfaction and fulfillment from your work in addition to income, retirement may simply be a comfortable safety net or supplement as you continue pursuing your passion.

Recently my father retired after working in an organization 56 years. At age 80 he decided to step aside, although he will still serve as chairman of the board for three additional years. Retirement for my father was a life decision, not a financial decision, as he could have financially retired at least 25 years sooner than he did. A proper retirement plan simply allowed my father to do the right thing at the right time for the right reasons.

This book will cause you to review, think and act. You spend many thousands of hours earning your living, a portion of which goes into your retirement. If you exchanged thousands of hours of your life to get something, it's certainly worth a bit of time and effort in the coming days to make sure that your money is working as hard for you as you worked for it.

In my work as an author, speaker, columnist, movie producer and television network owner, I meet thousands of people who represent every economic strata of society. These people all see money as different things. They may look at money as new cars, new clothes, luxurious vacations, children's college education, or any number of other things. In reality, money and a retirement fund represent nothing more or less than choices. Money and income give us options. These options are important during our working years, but become vital in retirement.

This book is designed to help you make the right decisions now so you will have the right choices later.

– Jim Stovall
Author, "The Ultimate Gift" and "The Lamp"
Emmy Award-winning TV producer

AUTHOR'S NOTE

"Retirement Held Hostage" is an eye-opening collection of innovative strategies to help retirees and aspiring retirees work toward a successful future. Bookstores are cluttered with many financial self-help books, but this guide to rescuing your retirement from bad advice is tested in the trenches of the heartland and provides real-world strategies by one of the top advisors in the country.

Readers are reminded that the concepts learned from this book are defined in a more general manner, and your individual circumstances may differ. When implementing the strategies herein, please note that there's no substitute for a well-equipped and expertly trained wealth advisor. To help you find and hire the right advice-giver I've included a handy step-by-step guide later in this book.

In addition, laws in this area are complex and always changing, so it's advisable to employ a qualified legal professional when updating your wealth plan. Last, but not least, regardless of what any financial professional tells you, there is no perfect investment. Every investment product has pros, cons and "strings attached," so be sure you understand these before investing.

CONTENTS

WHY MANY FAIL TO LIVE UP TO THEIR RETIREMENT DREAMS

"Getting to the summit is optional; getting down is mandatory."

– Ed Viesturs
Mount Everest climber

Is your retirement being held hostage? Are your retirement dreams being held back from reaching their peak potential? Do you believe there could be wiser, more effective ways to preserve and create wealth and take income in retirement?

If so, then you found the right book. Through my years working as a total wealth manager for affluent individuals, I've discovered that most advice given by advisors is bad advice. Unintentionally, of course, but bad nonetheless. Consequently, my goal of writing this book is to help you free your retirement by rescuing it from bad advice.

The first step in putting you back in control of your retirement is to help you focus on the right things. The things you can control. Far too often we focus on things we have no control over, like what goes on in Washington, Europe, or on Wall Street. Do these things affect your retirement? Sure, but you cannot control them. Let's focus on what you do have control of and make wise and informed decisions to get your retirement back on track and back in the black.

Each section of this book is laid out to help you conquer the bad advice that is holding back your retirement from its peak potential – be it over-taxation, antiquated investment strategies or the next big bubble.

Chances are, if you're reading this book you have a retirement nest egg worth preserving. Congratulations! The good news is that you're one of the few who has saved and planned carefully for one of the biggest events in life: retirement. The bad news is that you're only halfway through your journey of life, and this is where the most disastrous mistakes can happen to retirees and aspiring retirees.

You see, this is the point in their lives when most people stop planning. They think they've reached the

> **How long do you think Everest climbers prepare for the treacherous and potentially deadly journey? Do they focus on just the first half of their journey, the ascent? Or do they train, prepare and condition for the ascent AND the descent? How is this different from your financial preparation for and during retirement?**

finish line (retirement), and this is where their wealth plan "matures." They think that if they rebalance their investment portfolio, buy the right insurance, and have a will or living trust that they are set – they can just coast on autopilot. This couldn't be farther from the truth!

Your financial life is akin to climbing Mount Everest. Sounds weird, but it's true. Mount Everest is the highest mountain in the world (the size of 20 Empire State Buildings), which makes it the mecca for the most daring climbers. The difficulties of climbing Mount Everest are legendary: massive avalanches, hurricane-force winds, hypothermia from temperatures dipping to -76°F, mile-long crevasses and zero visibility snowstorms all lie in wait for unprepared or unlucky climbers.

How long do you think Everest climbers prepare for the treacherous and potentially deadly journey? Do they focus on just the first half of their journey, the ascent? Or do they train, prepare and condition for the ascent AND the descent? How is this different from your financial preparation for and during retirement?

If you can ascend the mountain, reach the peak and then descend – all without dying – you join the elite few. The same applies to your wealth plan. If you accumulate enough savings for retirement (ascending the mountain),

> **It's important to play a strong first half of your life, but it's all about the score at the end of your life that determines whether or not you and your family win or lose. What do you want the score to be at the end of your life? If you're ready to preserve and create more wealth in retirement, then read on, brave climber!**

enter retirement with a strategic income plan without the risk of outliving your money (the peak), and pass a legacy onto your family/charity without taxation/probate (the descent) – all without your wealth plan "dying" – then you, too, will join the elite few.

I'm sure you're no different than the clients I've helped over the past several years. They've come to me with a nice sum of money saved for their retirement years. They were proud of their accomplishment, financially independent and secure. Unfortunately that's where the problem lay. They were so focused on ascending Mount Everest (accumulating their nest egg), they had no plan for what to do when they reached the peak (retirement) and how to descend safely (preserving/distributing their nest egg).

Let me make another comparison for the football fans reading this book. Everyone in my family is a die-hard Ohio State Buckeye fan. (Go, Bucks!) When we huddle around the TV to watch a game, we pay little attention to the score at halftime. Loyal OSU fans know that the team has the uncanny ability to stink up the first half and rally during the second half. See, it's not the score at halftime that matters. It's the score at the end of the game that determines who wins and who loses.

Hopefully, the light bulb just went off in your mind. Retirement is halftime! It's important to play a strong first half of your life, but it's all about the score at the end of your life that determines whether or not you and your family win or lose.

What do you want the score to be at the end of your life? If you're ready to preserve and create more wealth in retirement, then read on, brave climber!

HOW BADLY DO YOU NEED A RETIREMENT RESCUE?

"There's very little advice in men's magazines, because men don't think there's a lot they don't know. Women do. Women want to learn. Men think, 'I know what I'm doing, just show me somebody naked.'"

– Jerry Seinfeld

How secure is your retirement plan? Are you prepared for the next bubble? Are you certain that you won't run out of money? Are there cracks in your tax strategy or estate plan that money could be falling through?

The following quiz addresses some of the biggest planning errors and mistakes I've seen aspiring retirees and retirees routinely make. Take this short quiz, grade your score, and discover your level of financial security.

1. When was the last time your advisor and attorney met to discuss your estate plan?

   _____ Never (2 points)

   _____ Years ago (1 point)

   _____ Within the last 12 months (0 points)

2. Within the last 10 years have you been unhappy with your investment returns?

   _____ Yes (2 points)

   _____ Kind of (1 point)

   _____ No (0 points)

3. Does your portfolio consist of only stocks, bonds, and/ or mutual funds?

   _____ Yes (1 point)

   _____ No (0 points)

4. When was the last time your advisor reviewed your tax return?

_____ Never (2 points)

_____ Years ago (1 point)

_____ Within the last 12 months (0 points)

5. Does your successor trustee know where to find your beneficiary designation forms?

_____ Yes (0 points)

_____ No (1 point)

6. Is the ultimate beneficiary of your IRA a trust?

_____ Yes (1 point)

_____ I don't know (1 point)

_____ No (0 points)

7. Are you worried about your family's financial well-being in the future?

_____ Yes (1 point)

_____ No (0 points)

8. Do you have a reliable income plan for retirement that guarantees you will not run out of money?

_____ Yes, I take 3% to 5% out every year (1 point)

_____ Yes, I have an income plan I cannot outlive (0 points)

_____ No, I don't (1 point)

9. If you died tomorrow, would your spouse have to live on a lower income amount?

_____ Yes (1 point)

_____ No (0 points)

_____ Unsure (2 points)

10. Do you have a diversified strategy to protect you from inflation?

_____ Yes (0 points)

_____ No (1 point)

11.Do you have investment losses you haven't used up on your tax return?

_____ Yes (1 point)

_____ No (0 points)

12. Are you currently paying a management fee on a portfolio of mutual funds?

_____ Yes (1 point)

_____ No (0 points)

13. Does your IRA include a variable annuity?

_____ Yes (1 point)

_____ No (0 points)

14. Is your advisor a recognized specialist in retirement accounts like IRAs, TSPs and 401(k)s?

_____ Yes (0 points)

_____ No (1 point)

15. Do you know the difference between A, B and C share mutual funds?

_____ Yes (0 points)

_____ No (1 point)

16. Are your retirement accounts set up to be a pension for your family?

_____ Yes (0 points)

_____ No (2 points)

_____ Unsure (1 point)

17. Are your kids' names on your bank accounts, brokerage accounts or property deeds?

_____ Yes (1 point)

_____ No (0 points)

18. Do you own bonds or bond funds?

_____ Yes (1 point)

_____ No (0 points)

19. Is your advisor a frequent contributor to the national financial media? (FOX Business, CNBC *The Wall Street Journal*, etc.)

_____ Yes (0 points)

_____ No (1 point)

20. Have you seen, in person, your financial advisor in the last 12 months?

____ Yes (0 points)

____ No (2 points)

____ I handle my investments (2 points)

Total Score ____

HOW DID YOU SCORE?

If you scored 10 or more points, you are almost certainly facing some form of significant financial problems, and you would likely benefit greatly from a second opinion from a qualified advice-giver.

If you scored 3 to 10 points, you may potentially be at risk for problems that could affect your income, your retirement security or your family wealth transfer goals. It may be wise, at this point, to seek a second opinion from a qualified advice-giver to help ensure that problems don't arise in the future.

If you scored less than 3 points, you are likely not exposed to severe planning mistakes that can have significant financial impact on you, your spouse and ultimately your family. Congratulations!

Chapter 1
BORN FREE, TAXED TO DEATH

"I'm putting all my money into taxes – the only thing sure to go up."

– Henny Youngman

To many retirees and aspiring retirees, "TAXES" is a four-letter word, and I understand why. You come into life paying taxes, and you certainly leave this world with a large tax bill. I believe this is all by design. The tax code is complex and difficult for a reason – to make it difficult for you and me! It seems like there are actually two different tax codes in the United States: one for the informed and one for the uninformed.

Who do you think pays more in taxes, the informed or the uninformed?

Ever heard the saying, "It's not about how much you earn, but how much you keep after taxes?" This couldn't be a more accurate statement, especially for retirees and their beneficiaries. This is one thing the ultra-wealthy do really well: They take advantage of the tax laws for the informed. How, you wonder? They have the right team (more on this in a later chapter).

I know you're probably thinking to yourself, "I use tax-prep software," or "I hired a fancy accountant," or "I'm a former IRS agent," or "I'm using all the latest tax-saving strategies." Are you? I can tell you with virtual certainty that you're probably paying more in taxes than you're obligated to.

I meet with prospective clients every week, and it's a rare occurrence that I can't find some way to put more money back in their pockets by lowering their tax bills. Look, millions of Americans are literally depending on you NOT to take advantage of the tax code for the informed!

Do you want to turn the tables on the government (legally and ethically, of course) and pay less taxes?

First, I think it's important to set the foundation for:

- Why taxes are set to skyrocket from where they are currently
- How massive tax rates will affect you
- And, most importantly, how to take advantage of the tax laws for the informed and pay the least amount in taxes now and in the future

Are you ready?

THE "GREAT WALL" OF DEBT

For most Americans, the income tax, capital gains tax, dividend tax, estate tax, FICA tax, Social Security income tax, sales tax, property tax, and tax on interest income (just to name a few) have almost always been part of everyday American life. It's almost as American as well... apple pie. OK, bad example.

But it hasn't always been this way. We haven't always been born free and taxed to death.

It was Feb. 3, 1913 when everything changed. The 16th amendment to the U.S. Constitution was ratified, giving Congress the power to tax personal income. At the time, less than 2% of the population had to pay income tax. But as we now know, this single ripple charted the course for decades of massive tax hikes and entitlement programs, and ultimately laid the foundation for a colossal amount of national debt that has never before been witnessed in our country's history – or the world's, for that matter.

In the informal public polls I've conducted over the last several years, there's an overwhelming common understanding that tax rates will go up, but why? Some point to Washington-style earmarks, some to the numerous entitlement programs like welfare and Social

> **About one-third of our country's spending will be used to pay the interest on our debt – not the principal – to our creditors! According to the Federal Reserve, over 50% of our national debt is owed to foreign nations, mostly China and Japan. Let that sink in for a moment.**

Security, while others point to the exploding national debt brought on by massive bailout and spending programs. The truth is that it's all of the reasons above, plus more.

The chart on the next page depicts the major components of federal spending. While defense accounts for 20% of all federal spending, Social Security and Medicare/Medicaid (all of which are entitlement programs) account for 40% of all federal spending.

The Social Security Administration (SSA) states that in 2010 it began operating at negative cash flow (paying out more in benefits than it takes in). Our national spending spree problem is exacerbated when we take a peek into the future. By the year 2040, Social Security, Medicare/Medicaid will account for 52% of all spending, while 30% will be attributed to the interest on our national debt.

About one-third of our country's spending will be used to pay the interest on our debt – not the principal – to our creditors! According to the Federal Reserve, over 50% of our national debt is owed to foreign nations, mostly China and Japan. Let that sink in for a moment.

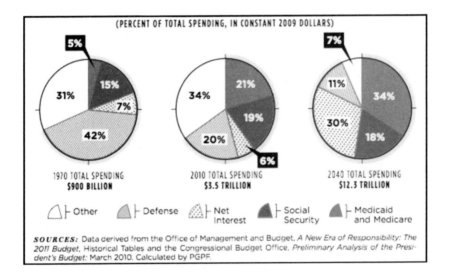

(PERCENT OF TOTAL SPENDING, IN CONSTANT 2009 DOLLARS)

| 1970 TOTAL SPENDING | 2010 TOTAL SPENDING | 2040 TOTAL SPENDING |
| **$900 BILLION** | **$3.5 TRILLION** | **$12.3 TRILLION** |

△⊢ Other   ⊿⊢ Defense   ⊿⊢ Net Interest   ⊿⊢ Social Security   ⊿⊢ Medicaid and Medicare

SOURCES: Data derived from the Office of Management and Budget, *A New Era of Responsibility: The 2011 Budget,* Historical Tables and the Congressional Budget Office, *Preliminary Analysis of the President's Budget:* March 2010. Calculated by PGPF.

I think you'll agree that the government has a spending problem comparable to a lottery winner with a nasty drug addiction. This is one habit that "we the people" need to encourage the government to kick before it overdoses.

Federal spending, however, is only part of the problem. The serious nature of the issue can be illustrated by a simple formula I devised:

ROBERT'S RULE

$$R - S = D$$

Revenue minus **S**pending
equals **D**ebt (accumulation)/surplus

To put it into perspective, current federal tax revenue is $2,168,454,559,411, and U.S federal spending is $3,480,644,561,058. Let's plug this information into my handy-dandy formula, $R - S = D$:

$$\$2,168,454,559,411 \text{ minus } \$3,480,644,561,058$$
$$\text{equals } (\$1,312,190,001,647)$$

This is so simple a fourth-grader can comprehend it, but for some reason it's difficult for a politician. The beauty is that this formula, like gravity, is undeniable and applies to our everyday lives. If you spend more than you collect,

> **While it's easy to talk about trillions and trillions of dollars of debt, it's very difficult to conceptualize how much $1 trillion really is. To put it into perspective, if you spent $1 million each day, it would take you 2,700 years to spend $1 trillion.**

you accumulate debt. And the opposite is true. If you spend less than you collect, you cut debt – or even better, create a surplus.

So, using the formula above, we are running a deficit and growing our national debt by over $1.3 trillion a year, a record-breaking pace. You can see on the next page how dramatic the gap is between spending and tax revenues.

Because the government is and has been spending more than it receives in tax revenue, we've been tallying up quite a bar tab. While it's easy to talk about trillions

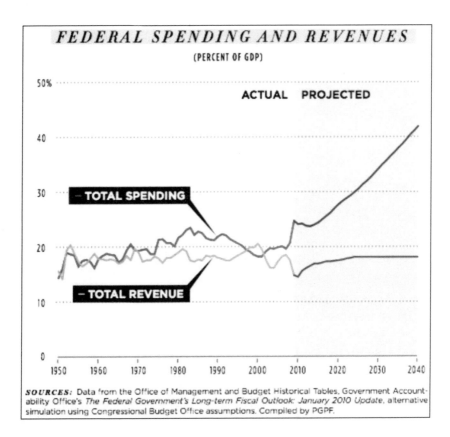

FEDERAL SPENDING AND REVENUES
(PERCENT OF GDP)

ACTUAL   PROJECTED

TOTAL SPENDING

TOTAL REVENUE

SOURCES: Data from the Office of Management and Budget Historical Tables, Government Account-ability Office's *The Federal Government's Long-term Fiscal Outlook: January 2010 Update*, alternative simulation using Congressional Budget Office assumptions. Compiled by PGPF.

and trillions of dollars of debt, it's very difficult to concep-tualize how much $1 trillion really is. To put it into per-spective, if you spent $1 million each day, it would take 2,700 years to spend $1 trillion.

The question I'm hoping you've formed in your mind is, "Why not raise taxes and cut spending to solve the problem?" Good question, young grasshopper! Unfortu-nately, the accumulated debt is too large and the entitle-ment promises too great to make a significant dent in our "great wall" of debt.

At the time this book was authored, the national debt was over $15 trillion and, according to USDebtClock.org, the unfunded liabilities (current and future promises) of

U.S. National Debt

In Trillions of Dollars, Source: Treasury Department

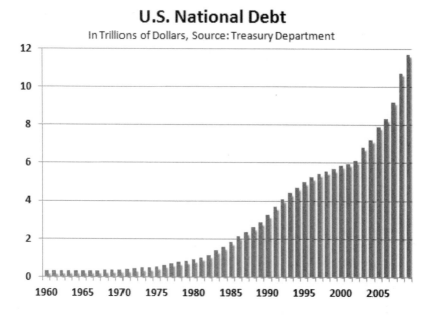

Social Security and Medicare/Medicaid are a staggering $112 trillion. How much does the government have put away to keep its promises?

Zero.

What will the government do? The non-partisan Peter G. Peterson Foundation answers this question more eloquently than I could:

> *"It's much easier to expand government programs and provide tax cuts, reap the short-term political benefits, and then let future politicians – and citizens – deal with the consequences."*

Social Security is a perfect example of a program that has been pillaged by politicians since its inception in 1935. According to the CBO (Congressional Budget Office), Social Security is already running a $45 billion deficit, five years earlier than anticipated. This means that Social Security is paying more out in benefits than it collects in tax revenue. Furthermore, the Social Security Administration recently found that Social Security "trust funds" will be completely exhausted by 2033. Could this shortfall affect your retirement? Possibly. Could this shortfall affect your grandchildren's retirement? I think the answer is obvious.

The overwhelming conclusion is the U.S. cannot keep entitlement promises and lower tax rates. The perfect storm is brewing right above Washington, D.C. In the not so distant future there will be a great divide between the "haves" and the "have nots" – in essence, a new Civil War. In other words, there will be a great divide between those who saved for retirement and accumulated family wealth, and those who are dependent on the federal government.

To put it bluntly, the dam is about to break. Do you want your family and future generations to be caught in the flood?

Politicians will keep spending your money and use the spending spree as a springboard to raise taxes as the only solution to the debt problem. That's why you'll need to be ahead of the curve by taking advantage of the tax laws for the informed, and this book will be your guide.

THERE'S ALWAYS A SILVER LINING

The stage has been set for skyrocketing tax rates, but the silver lining is they haven't skyrocketed yet. Tax rates are still relatively low, so now is the time to do some smart tax planning and take advantage of the tax laws for the informed.

In 2011 and 2012 tax rates remained low because of the Obama administration extending the original tax cuts put into place in 2001 and 2003 during the Bush administration. Following is a breakdown of tax rates as they stand now:

2011/2012 FEDERAL TAX BRACKETS	
Tax Bracket	**Married Filing Jointly**
10% Bracket	$0 - $16,750
15% Bracket	$16,750 - $68,000
25% Bracket	$68,000 - $137,300
28% Bracket	$137,300 - $209,250
33% Bracket	$209,250 - $373,650
35% Bracket	$373,650+

From my experience, the majority of retired couples fall within the 15% or 25% tax brackets, meaning they make somewhere between $35,000 and $135,000 per year. Keep this point in mind as you witness what will take place in 2013 when the Bush-era tax cuts are automatically repealed.

At the top of the next page is a breakdown of the new tax rates for 2013 and beyond. Where did the 10% and 25% brackets go? I thought the Bush tax cuts were for the wealthy! They were. And they were for everyone else,

2013 AND BEYOND FEDERAL TAX BRACKETS	
Tax Bracket	**Married Filing Jointly**
15% Bracket	$0 - $43,850
28% Bracket	$43,850 - $105,950
31% Bracket	$105,950 - $161,450
36% Bracket	$161,450 - $288,350
39.6% Bracket	$288,350+

too, especially middle-income earners. The 10% and 25% brackets disappear in 2013, and the other tax brackets get compressed.

Now let's look below at a side-by-side comparison of current tax rates vs. tax increases in 2013:

FEDERAL TAX BRACKETS NOW vs. 2013 AND BEYOND			
Rate	**2011-2012**	**Rate**	**2013 and Beyond**
10%	$0 - $16,750	NA	No 10% Bracket
15%	$16,750 - $68,000	15%	$0 - $43,850
25%	$68,000 - $137,300	28%	$43,850 - $105,950
28%	$137,300 - $209,250	31%	$105,950 - $161,450
33%	$209,250 - $373,650	36%	$161,450 - $288,350
35%	$373,650+	39.6%	$288,350+

Wow! I bet our founding fathers are rolling over in their graves! I can imagine George Washington saying, "We left England for this?"

What does this mean to the average retired couple who make somewhere between $35,000 and $135,000 per year? They're forced to give the government a raise – and a hefty raise at that!

Retired couples who are currently in the 15% bracket (making $44,000 or more) will in effect see a doubling of their tax rate, from 15% to 28%. And those retired couples who are currently in the 25% bracket (making $68,000 or more) will see their tax rate increase by 24%.

Hopefully I've coached you well enough early on in this book to recognize that smart, informed retirees can pay less in taxes than those above.

There are really two ways to take advantage of the tax laws for the informed, now and in the future. Read on.

Chapter 2
HOW THE ULTRA-WEALTHY PAY LESS TAX THAN YOU

"The income tax has made more liars out of the American people than golf has."

– Will Rogers

There's a big difference between tax evasion and tax avoidance. One you go to jail for, and the other shows you're taking advantage of the tax laws for the informed. I'll give you a hint: One commonality of the ultra-wealthy is that they've assembled the right team of advisors to help them avoid unnecessary taxation.

With tax rates set to skyrocket, what are the ultra-wealthy doing to pay less taxes? I'll give you a sneak-peak.

HOW TO SAVE ON TAXES NOW
AND IN THE FUTURE

There are four really big tax strategies I think you should consider implementing immediately:

Strategy #1
TAKE THE GAIN AND RUN

I remember during the last bull market I had met with a few prospective clients who had significant long-term gains in stocks, real estate or other investments. Inevitably the conversation would stall when it came to the discussion of taking the gain. "I don't want to sell ABC stock because I'll owe taxes on the gain." In essence, the IRS had paralyzed them from making a smart decision about their money. I wonder how much they regret not taking the gain (before it was wiped out by the great recession) and paying the small tax owed to the IRS.

Let their poor judgment be a lesson for you. When evaluating the sale of an investment, your tax burden should be part of your consideration, but certainly not the only consideration. When it's time to change investments, it's time to change investments. As Mark Twain said:

> *"Twenty years from now, you will be more disappointed by the things that you didn't do than by the ones you did do..."*

I'm not claiming Mark Twain was suggesting for you to take investment gains when you have them. I think he was a little more concerned with writing books than figuring the tax bill on long-term capital gains. I do, however, believe you should consider locking in your gains while capital gains rates are historically low.

The current max federal capital gains rate is 15%. What will it be in 2013? How about 33% higher than it is

> **When evaluating the sale of an investment, your tax burden should be part of your consideration, but certainly not the only consideration. When it's time to change investments, it's time to change investments.**

now? What if you could pay 33% less than you would in the near future?

Listen, I believe that capital gains rates are on sale – heck I'd even consider them to be in the clearance bin! The only time in U.S. history when these rates were lower was from 1922 to 1933.[1]

The best part is, you may even qualify for a 0% capital gains rate if you're in the 10% or 15% tax bracket (see previous chapter for tax bracket information).

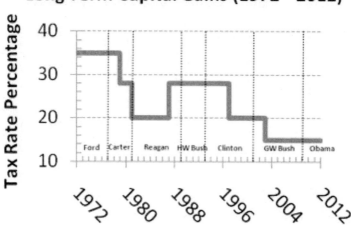

I cannot tell you how many tax returns I've reviewed where the person had massive carry-over losses from the last market downturn, while their investment statements show unrealized gains. (Carry-over losses are investment losses that haven't been used up, so they get carried over to the next tax year.)

Losses offset gains, dollar for dollar, so why wouldn't you cash in some gains tax-free and get some use from those losses? Money is falling through the cracks! If you don't have gains you can take to use up carry-over losses, then shouldn't you have a strategy to create gains? Advisors and investors often miss this critical point.

One of my favorite questions to ask people in this scenario is, "When was the last time your current advisor reviewed your tax return?" Ninety-nine percent of the time they say, "My advisor has never asked to see my tax return." Why not? How could you possibly be taking advantage of the tax laws for the informed? The biggest tax disasters I see happen right under the advisor's nose, and the previous example is no exception. Shouldn't the financial hand know what the tax hand is doing?

Let me ask you a question, dear reader: When was the last time your advisor asked to see a copy of your tax

> **When was the last time your advisor asked to see a copy of your tax return? If your answer is anywhere from "never," to "years ago," consider this your wake-up call. You're not taking advantage of the tax laws for the informed.**

return? If your answer is anywhere from "never," to "years ago," consider this your wake-up call. You're not taking advantage of the tax laws for the informed.

Strategy #2
THE TAX-EFFICIENT FRONTIER

Most men carry a wallet. Some carry a purse, but that's a whole other book. Most men carry their wallet in the same pocket every day. Personally, I feel it's more comfortable in my left pocket. If I have a hole in my preferred pocket, I reposition my wallet to the other pocket, and it, well, feels uncomfortable. It feels kind of unnatural. (Ladies, stay with me here. Trust me, there's a point to my story.)

What happens when you have a hole in your pocket? You have to move your wallet to the other pocket so you don't lose any money through the hole. Guess what? You probably have holes in your investments that money is

Not Tax-Efficient	Tax-Efficient
Mutual Funds	Managed Stocks/ETFs
Corporate Bonds	Municipal Bonds
CDs	Deferred Annuities
Savings & Money Markets	Life Insurance Proceeds

falling through in the form of unnecessary taxes. What should you do? Change pockets!

I know you're probably thinking, "But that's uncomfortable, I don't want to change pockets." You're right, change is rarely comfortable, but that's no reason not to do something, especially when you're losing money. It's time to consider repositioning your investments to take advantage of the tax laws for the informed. It's time to put that wallet in the other pocket.

The chart above categorizes the most common investments by tax-efficiency. Let's take it line by line.

> **Please note:** *This is not a discussion on investment performance, but one could draw the conclusion that greater tax-efficiency could translate into higher investment returns, especially for high-income earners. This is known as the tax-adjusted return, but I digress.*

Mutual funds vs. managed stocks/exchange traded funds (ETFs) – Many mutual fund investors will be surprised to know they may be losing a good chunk of their return to the taxman. According to Morningstar.com:

> *"[Mutual] fund investors are at a disadvantage when it comes to taxes…investors in conventional mutual funds can get stuck with a tax bill on their mutual fund holdings, even if they've lost money since they've held the fund."*

I call this a "double-whammy," because one of my favorite TV game shows of the '80s was "Press Your Luck." I loved the little whammy character, as he would take the contestants' winnings in an amusing way if they landed on his space (although I'm sure the contestants were less than thrilled).

What's a mutual fund double-whammy? Losing money in a fund because of a bad year in the market, then getting a tax bill on capital gains even though you didn't gain anything.

Mutual fund managers have the difficult responsibility of pleasing current investors while pleasing their marketing department by posting returns that attract new investors. Because of this dual mandate, negative years in the market will typically compel the fund manager to sell an underlying investment that has a gain in order to lower the overall loss in the fund. Voila! You get a tax bill for capital gains. The industry term for this is "window-dressing," and it's a nauseating drawback of mutual funds.

TAKE THE BUS OR A LIMO?

Mutual funds are like mass transit. It's not tailored to you; you get on with everyone else and you get off with everyone else. If you're concerned with lowering taxes

> **If you're concerned with lowering taxes (using the tax laws for the informed), know that conventional mutual funds are one of the least tax-efficient vehicles known to man.**

(using the tax laws for the informed), know that conventional mutual funds are one of the least tax-efficient vehicles known to man.

If you're comfortable with the ups and downs of the market, a professionally managed stock/ETF portfolio can be more tax-efficient than conventional mutual funds, because the tax strategy is tailored to your personal sensitivity to taxes. It's like riding in a limo compared to the city bus. Which would you rather take?

As an added tax-saving bonus, you may even be able to deduct the management fee charged by your professional money manager. Good-bye, whammy; hello, tax-efficiency!

Corporate bonds vs. municipal bonds – Bond investors buy bonds because they enjoy the fixed income aspect (aka yield) and no stock market risk (except in the case of bond funds*). There may also be an added benefit in the form of tax savings for some specific types of bonds. Corporate bonds offer no tax shelter, because the interest income is subject to both federal and state income tax.

Conversely, municipal bond interest is tax-free at the federal level, and if the bond is issued within the state you live, it's also state income tax-free. However, the interest you earn may cause you to be subject to the alternative minmum tax (AMT) and/or cause your Social Security income to become taxable.

Because of their tax-efficiency, municipal bonds pay a lower yield when compared with corporate bonds. This tax break can be huge if you're in a high tax bracket. The best way to evaluate the benefit of buying a tax-free municipal bond vs. a taxable corporate bond is to calculate what's called the tax-equivalent yield.

ROBERT'S RULE

Muni yield divided by
(1 minus your federal tax bracket) equals
tax-equivalent yield.

Using this formula, suppose you have a municipal bond paying a 5% yield, and you're in the 28% tax bracket:

5% divided by (1 minus 0.28) equals 6.94%

So, 6.94% is the tax-equivalent yield of the municipal bond, which is helpful to know when comparing a

---

*See additional bond risk table in Chapter 3.

tax-free bond to a taxable bond. All things being equal (bond rating, maturity date, etc.), you would need a taxable bond to yield more than 6.94% to make it worthwhile for consideration.

> **Please note:** *All too often I've seen other advisors misuse and abuse municipal bonds by putting them in the portfolios of clients who had no business being invested in them. Generally speaking, you shouldn't even consider this strategy unless you're in a 28% tax bracket or higher, because you'll just be subjecting yourself to a low yield. Always use the tax-equivalent yield formula to compare apples to apples and not fall victim to the allure of "tax-free."*

CDs vs. deferred annuities – CDs (certificates of deposit) over the years have earned the nickname "certificates of disappointment," because of their shameful return and terrible tax-efficiency. The interest you earn on a CD is fully taxable, so you give up a large part of your return to the taxman.

If you have a $100,000 CD paying 1.50%, you earn $1,500 in interest over the year. If you're in the 28% tax bracket you give up $420 in taxes, so the "real return" of the CD is 1.08% after taxes. (This does not include the effect of inflation, which would put the "real return" of the CD into negative territory).

I'm sure you think of Michael Jackson when you think of CDs, right? You don't? I do, because of Michael's famous dance move, the "moonwalk." He looked like he was moving forward, but he was actually moving backward. That's why I think of the late King of Pop when I think of CDs. You look like you're moving forward, because you're making money; but after taxes and inflation you're actually moving backward. So, what you have is Michael Jackson CDs!

Faithful CD owners love their CDs, mostly because of the principal protection they offer. Deferred annuity owners also love their annuities, mostly because of the principal protection they offer (in the case of fixed annuities)[2]. But they also offer another significant benefit: They're far more tax-efficient.

Interest earned on a deferred annuity is tax-deferred (like an IRA), which offers protection from federal income taxes, state income taxes, and Social Security income taxes. So, like an IRA, a deferred annuity offers triple tax

> **That's why I think of the late King of Pop when I think of CDs. You look like you're moving forward, because you're making money; but after taxes and inflation you're actually moving backward. So, what you have is Michael Jackson CDs!**

deferral, which over time can add up to tremendous tax savings. The chart on the next page shows this tax-saving strategy in action, assuming a $100,000 deposit growing 6% annually for 12 years with a 28% tax bracket.

Year	Taxable @ 28%	Tax-Deferred
1	$104,320	$106,000
2	108,827	112,360
3	113,528	119,102
4	118,432	126,248
5	123,549	133,823
6	128,886	141,852
7	134,454	150,363
8	140,262	159,385
9	146,322	168,948
10	152,643	179,085
11	159,237	189,830
12	166,116	201,220

After 12 years in this tax-deferred annuity, you have
$35,104 more than the taxable account because of the
triple tax deferral. That's 21% more money in your pocket!
Part of the power of this strategy is understanding that not
only are your principal and interest compounding, but so
is the money that you would have normally paid taxes on.

What happens when the money comes out of a
deferred annuity? The growth on the annuity is taxed as
income (like an IRA), which is why many high-income
earners use deferred annuities as one of their preferred
retirement savings tools.

Savings and money markets vs. life insurance proceeds – Savings and money market accounts share the same tax-inefficiency that CDs do. Any interest earned is fully taxable, which can be a big chunk of your growth. I call excessive amounts in savings and money markets "lazy money," which I define as:

> **Lazy money,** *n.* 1. Money that's lying around all day long, doing absolutely nothing, sitting on the couch, eating Doritos, and watching a Jerry Springer marathon. 2. Money that's earning nothing and you're paying tax on it.

What if you could put some of this lazy money to work and convert it from taxable to tax-free? One idea is take a relatively small amount of lazy money and parlay it into a much larger amount of tax-free money.

One of the few major tax breaks that the IRS gives you is the tax-free benefit on life insurance proceeds. Life insurance has been around since the 17th century, but people to this day are still surprised to hear about the tax-free death benefit that it offers! It's all about taking advantage of the tax laws for the informed.

> **Please note:** There is tremendous controversy surrounding the various types of life insurance. To set the record straight, insurance is NOT an investment[2], nor should it be viewed as one. Life insurance is designed purely as an asset-protection tool with tremendous tax benefits when used correctly.

Strategy #3
TAX ME NOW OR TAX ME LATER

Suppose your rich great uncle left you a large inheritance, but you had to choose between receiving $1 million or $850,000. You're no dummy; you would go for the cool million, right?

But let's make this scenario a little more interesting. Suppose the $1 million is fully taxable as ordinary income, but the $850,000 is completely tax-free. Now which would you choose? Obviously, $850,000 tax-free would be worth far more than $1 million after taxes. Depending on the state where you live, you could easily see the $1 million reduced by 40%, leaving you with $600,000.

Most of our nation's wealth is tied up in accounts like the $1 million above, specifically in IRAs and other tax-deferred retirement plans such as 401(k)s, 403(b)s, TSPs, TSAs, PSPs and deferred compensation, to name just a few. The dangerous word here is tax-deferred, because for decades you've religiously contributed to your retirement plan and received an income tax deduction.

You've had a plan for accumulating money into your retirement plan, but what's your plan when the money comes out? The IRS has a plan, do you?

In essence, the IRS has an ownership interest in your tax-deferred retirement accounts, because you have to pay them off before you get anything. It's inevitable that at some point this great passage of wealth will be taxed, so the question becomes, would you rather pay tax now (while tax rates are low), or later (when tax rates are set to be higher)?

That's the beauty of a Roth conversion. You can lock in today's low tax rates on all or a portion of your tax-deferred retirement accounts. Let me be more specific:

> **That's the beauty of a Roth conversion. You can lock in today's low tax rates on all or a portion of your tax-deferred retirement accounts. Let me be more specific: Turn a *forever* income tax into a *never* income tax!**

Turn a *forever* income tax into a *never* income tax! Pay off the IRS now and position your retirement and the legacy you leave behind to grow income tax-free.

Remember the previous example about the rich great uncle? $850,000 tax-free is far more valuable than $1 million taxable.

On the next page, review the chart of "delayed pain," which compares paying the tax on retirement accounts now by converting to Roth, vs. delaying the pain and paying the tax in retirement.

You can see that the tax bill grows quickly over a rather short period of time. The longer the time frame, the better the Roth conversion works out for you. For some retirees planning to pass their Roths to their loved ones, the math looks really impressive!

You can see from the chart that you can pay the tax bill now, an estimated $25,000, vs. paying the bill later – an estimated $66,402 (after scheduled tax increases),

Age	Tax-Deferred Growth @ 6%	Tax Now vs. Tax Later
55	$100,000	$25,000 (@ 25%)
56	$106,000	
57	$112,360	
58	$119,101	
59	$126,247	
60	$133,822	
61	$141,851	
62	$150,363	
63	$159,384	
64	$168,947	
65	$179,084	
66	$189,829	
67	$201,219	$66,402 (@ 33%)

Please note: Most retirees do not take a lump sum upon retiring, but this is an illustration of the tax impact of delaying the inevitable.

a savings of $41,402. This is no small amount of money. Could you use an extra $41,402 in retirement to travel? Help a grandchild pay for college? Renovate your home?

With tax rates at historic lows for a limited time, there's a unique opportunity to convert your tax-deferred retirement account into a tax-free

retirement account, the Roth IRA. Some cringe at
the thought of paying taxes on the conversion to

**Some cringe at the thought of paying taxes
on the conversion to Roth, but
it may not be as painful as you think.**

Roth, but it may not be as painful as you think.
Consider the example below of a married couple
earning $80,000 per year, either paying the tax now

$ Conversion of IRA to Roth	Federal Tax Owed	Effective Federal Tax Rate
$0	$0	15%
$40,000	$9,327	23.2%
$60,000	$14,327	23.88%
$80,000	$19,467	24.56%
$100,000	$25,647	25.65%
$150,000	$39,949	26.63%
$200,000	$56,449	28.22%

to convert to Roth, or delaying the inevitable tax bill
(assuming current tax rates).

It's impressive to note that you can convert
$200,000 without doubling your effective federal tax
rate. But I think one of the better approaches for converting to Roth is the Roth rollout. Using this strategy,
you slowly convert your traditional IRA to Roth every
year while maintaining your current tax bracket.

Are Roth conversions the best thing since sliced bread and Pop Rocks? Hardly. Roth conversions are not for everyone; there are just as many reasons why you shouldn't convert as there are reasons why you should. Following are just a few:

Why You Shouldn't	Why You Should
If you need access to the money within the next five years.	If you want to take advantage of low tax rates and remove uncertainty about future tax rates.
If you don't have funds outside the IRA to pay the taxes on the conversion.	If you want to leave a tax-free legacy for your spouse, kids and grandkids.
If you plan to leave your IRAs to charities.	If you want to control when you take withdrawals (no forced required distributions).

While there are differing camps on this debate, I believe the number one reason why you shouldn't do a Roth conversion is if you don't have funds outside the IRA to pay the income tax on the conversion. The last thing you want to do is withhold taxes from the IRA to convert to a Roth, thus reducing its value.

For example, if you want to convert $100,000 of your IRA and you withhold 25% for taxes, your "new" Roth is only worth $75,000. It will take years to gain back the "lost" $25,000. Instead of withholding taxes, look for possible sources to pay the conversion tax, including bank accounts and CDs ("lazy money") or brokerage accounts (stocks and funds).

Strategy #4
THE "SUPER ROTH"

What's better than a tax-free Roth? A Roth with a cape – I call it a "Super Roth!"

You're now up to speed on Roth conversions, so let's take your knowledge to the next level: wealth conversions.

What if you could take a small amount of taxable wealth, for example $10,000, and turn it into $500,000 of tax-free wealth. Would you do it? From this hypothetical example, can you see the benefit of converting taxable wealth into tax-free wealth?

As a wealth advisor to my clients, it's my responsibility to both create AND preserve wealth during up and down markets. But if I am to be honest with myself, there's an area I used to be weak in, and that's wealth conversions.

> **What if you could take a small amount of taxable wealth, for example $10,000, and turn it into $500,000 of tax-free wealth. Would you do it?**

I can attest that it's wonderful to give clients peace of mind that even during recessions their retirement is secure. Yet if the majority of their retirement savings is tied up in tax-deferred accounts (IRAs, 401(k)s, etc.), there's another problem lurking for them and their family. Let me give you an example.

Say a client entrusted me with their $1 million IRA, and five years later their IRA is worth $1.4 million. I've done a great job creating and preserving their wealth, but what about passing the wealth on? Someone in their family will have to pay taxes on $1.4 million instead of $1 million, so how good of a job have I done? We're talking about $490,000 in taxes, a difference of $140,000 in lost wealth in only five years!

Then it hit me. Why not convert a small amount of wealth now into larger amount of tax-free wealth later? Upon further research, I found a small section of the IRS code (IRS 7702) that allows this wealth conversion. Hello, "Super Roth!"

Using this strategy we can convert a small portion of the $1.4 million IRA, say only 2% (or $28,000) every year, and parlay it into $1 million tax-free wealth above and beyond the IRA. At age 70, the IRS forces you to start taking out 3.65% annually as a required minimum distribution (RMD); so why not beat them at their game? (There are several other benefits to this strategy, but let's stay focused on the benefit of tax-free wealth.)

It sounds too good to be true, doesn't it? Understand that to implement this strategy you have to be healthy (generally only one out of three people qualify), and all this tax-free wealth doesn't benefit you directly, because the "Super Roth" must be funded with permanent life insurance.

IS LIFE INSURANCE A GOOD DEAL?

For years life insurance has had a well-deserved black eye. Even I was resistant to the concept until I did my own homework and implemented a "Super Roth" for my family. I say life insurance has had well-deserved black eye, because like most financial tools it has, at times, been misused, abused and oversold.

Will the life insurance agent make a good commission? Yes, which is why it should be designed with the lowest premium possible. Are there cheaper types of life insurance, like term life? Yes. But, this doesn't discount the use of properly designed permanent

ROBERT'S RULE

Simply put, term life insurance is for temporary problems; permanent life insurance is for permanent problems.

life, because term life won't get the job done. Term is temporary, and we need the insurance there when your family needs it. Simply put, term life insurance is for temporary problems; permanent life insurance is for permanent problems.

One of my goals for my clients is to keep the wealth in their family where it belongs. I believe it's critical to design this strategy with this goal in mind and minimally fund the life insurance policy. Why make the insurance company wealthy?

Bonus Strategy
NATURAL RESOURCE EXPLORATION (NRE) TAX SHELTERS

Did you take a big gain on an investment this year or exercise some stock options? Are you going to be in a high tax bracket? Maybe you took a large RMD from your IRAs or converted an IRA to Roth?

Would you like to shelter some of the above from taxes? An investment into natural resource exploration may do the trick.

Direct investments into natural resource exploration (NREs), such as drilling for oil, extracting natural gas, wind turbine installations or solar power

> **Direct investments into natural resource exploration (NREs), such as drilling for oil, extracting natural gas, wind turbine installations or solar power farming, may provide a large up-front tax write-off to offset your taxable income.**

farming, may provide a large up-front tax write-off to offset your taxable income. These long-term investments generally offer a tax shelter of between 70% to 100% of your initial investment.

In other words, if the NRE investment offers a 100% tax write-off, it reduces your taxable income for every dollar invested. On the next page is an illustration of a married couple filing jointly.

Without NRE	NRE With 100% Shelter
$150,000 Income	$150,000 Income ($75,000 Write-Off) $75,000 Income
($42,000) 28% Fed ($7,500) 5% State	($18,750) 25% Fed ($3,750) 5% State
$49,500 in Taxes	**$22,500 in Taxes** *A savings of $27,000*

Are you wondering why an NRE investor would receive such a generous tax break? Because the government is encouraging risk. Seriously. Whether it's real estate or NRE investing, the tax code contains provisions that offer tax breaks for risk-taking.

There are costs associated with "harvesting" the natural resource, whether it's drilling, land clearing, installation of equipment, etc.; and it's this cost that creates the tax shelter.

I GET A GENEROUS TAX BREAK, SO WHAT'S THE RISK?

Like all good things in life, this approach does not come without some level of risk. When you invest in an NRE, you invest as a general partner (GP) during the exploration phase. As one of the partners, you share not only in the tax write-off, but also in the liability if there are any accidents during the exploration process.

This is why it's critical to invest in an NRE that has a short exploration phase, successful operating history, AND one that has generous liability insurance (ideally $10 million to $20 million in coverage). Once the exploration phase is complete (ideally in one year or less), your liability diminishes dramatically as the GPs are converted to LPs (limited partners). The important consideration is that you shouldn't invest your rainy day money in an NRE, as they are generally long-term, illiquid investments.

TAX SHELTERS, CASH FLOW, AND INFLATION AND MARKET HEDGES

Successful NRE investors use these vehicles not only as a tax shelter, but also for the ample cash flow and as a hedge against inflation and stock market risk.

Generally, the NREs we've utilized have a fairly conservative goal of 8% percent to 10% cash flow per year, once the exploration phase is complete. That can be a great complement to a retirement income plan. With that said, NREs aren't available to just anyone. Typically you have to qualify as an accredited investor: someone who is a high-income earner or has saved $1 million or more in liquid assets.

As you'll soon discover in an upcoming chapter, it's critical to the success of your retirement dreams to NOT have everything invested in the market, AND to protect your income from the sneaky, but devastating, effects of inflation. NREs have no correlation to the whims of a volatile stock market, and they are a classic inflation hedge, specifically oil and natural gas NREs. As oil and natural gas prices rise over time due to inflation, so goes the cash flow of your NRE investment.

Not all NREs are created equal, so do your homework and hire an advisor who knows these investments inside and out. If it doesn't pass the "smell test," don't invest. It's best to allocate some of your funds to NREs and invest over a period of years to diversify their high-risk profiles. By prudently reviewing NREs you may be rewarded with generous tax shelters, ample cash flow, insulation from a volatile market, and a valuable inflation hedge.

AN IMPORTANT CONSIDERATION

The thing I want you to think about, and I cannot stress this enough, is that when you're weighing a strategy that may create a significant tax bill, do your homework. Always meet with your tax advisor and run a "dummy" tax return.

Any time you introduce additional income into your tax return, it's like releasing the ball on a pinball machine – all kinds of bells and whistles go off. That's what you need to do here, too. Put the additional income into your return and see what bells and whistles go off. For example, does it cause your Social Security income to become taxable? What does it do to your alternative minimum tax?

Most importantly, you should be working with an advisor who is proactively working with your tax advisor to discuss strategies like the ones I've outlined here.

Be wise by taking advantage of the tax laws for the informed, but do it prudently!

Chapter 3
RESCUING YOUR RETIREMENT FROM TOXIC ECONOMICS

"I, however, place economy among the first and most important republican virtues, and public debt as the greatest of the dangers to be feared."

– Thomas Jefferson

I'll be the first to admit that I was a sub-par college student when it came to economics classes. I would be willing to wager that if I were to tell my economics professors that my opinion is well respected by *The Wall Street Journal*, Fox Business and CNBC, they would, well, laugh.

So it's no surprise that in my college years I didn't find economics interesting. To me, it was a boring subject that lacked passion, simplicity and real-life application. This belief changed, of course, when I discovered ways to inject passion, simplicity and real-life applications to everyday economics. Economics means different things to different people. What I had to figure out was, what does it mean to me? And, more importantly, how does it apply to my clients' wealth?

> **What the field of economics allowed my team and me to do is filter for opportunities to create wealth and potentially avoid disasters. This is what I term *economic arbitrage*.**

Economics can't help you to time the stock market, like many claim. No one can time the market. I can't. You can't. So why are you or your advisor trying? (That's a whole different book.)

What the field of economics allowed my team and me to do is filter for opportunities to create wealth and potentially avoid disasters. This is what I term *economic arbitrage*.

Carefully wrapped in this chapter, I believe, are three of the most important and crucial concepts to understand when it comes to rescuing your retirement from toxic economics.

It's up to you. Only you can determine your future as the gap widens between those who live their ideal retirement and those who cannot. I believe that brokers and advisors across the nation are unaware, unprepared, or have become complacent:

They say stocks are cheap; it's time to buy.

They say buying stocks is the best way to make money.

They say it's just a paper loss, it will come back.

They say that "buy, hold and pray" works.

They say bonds are the safest investment.

They say a portfolio of stocks and bonds is the best way to diversify your money.

They say you can take 3% to 4% out of your investments for income and you shouldn't run out of money in retirement.

I say this is lazy and absolutely irresponsible advice.

The 21st century is all about Americans taking control of their financial future. It's all about individual responsibility and choice. It's all about you taking back control of your future.

The government is in over its head in debt. Pensions are disappearing left and right. The burden of rescuing your retirement rests squarely on your shoulders. But don't let your heart be troubled, because you are about to discover the three most important financial lessons for retirees and aspiring retirees. These once closely guarded

> **From a market historian's perspective, it's uncanny how the market has provided evidence of a series of boom/bust cycles every 20 or so years.**

economic arbitrage tools are now at your disposal. Use them wisely.

But first a history lesson...

THE DEFINITION OF INSANITY

Einstein defined insanity as doing the same thing over and over again and expecting different results. I don't know about you, but I think Einstein was a pretty smart guy.

While Santayana was no Einstein, he is well known for a quote that is complimentary to Einstein's definition of insanity:

> *"Those that cannot remember the past are condemned to repeat it."*

Is the person managing your hard-earned retirement savings heeding the sage wisdom of Einstein and Santayana?

Probably not. Here's why: You have or have been told to invest 60% or more of your irreplaceable wealth into stocks or mutual funds – at quite possibly the worst time historically.

Brokers and advisors regurgitate the same mantras. You've heard them before. They say things like, "The market always comes back." And you know what? They're right. The market does come back, given enough time. But why subject your retirement dreams and lifestyle to this insanity?

BOOM AND BUST MARKET CYCLES OVER THE LAST 80+ YEARS

From a market historian's perspective it's uncanny how the market has provided evidence of a series of boom/bust cycles every 20 or so years.

During the Great Gatsby era of the Roaring '20s, America was in a growth mode like never before. People bought furs, more could afford these newfangled contraptions called cars, and even more poured money into the stock market. Of course, the Great Depression changed all of that in 1929.

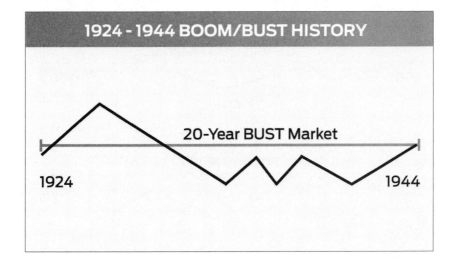

Once WWII ended in 1945, Americans got busy again, both at work and at home. Enter the baby boom generation and a 20-year period of growth and prosperity.

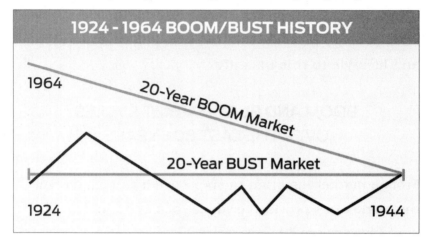

Next was a polar opposite market. During the '60s, the Beatles invaded the United States, the Vietnam War greatly escalated, and "flower power" flourished as peace, love and happiness took hold, and the markets went into hibernation once again for an 18-year period.

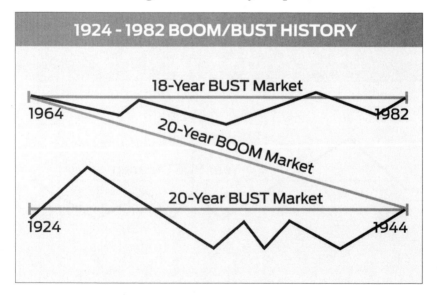

The '80s and '90s marked a new era in the United States. The age of information exploded as Microsoft, Apple and IBM introduced personal hardware and software, and Internet companies such as Google, Amazon and other dot-coms became household names. The technology bubble seemingly developed overnight and out of sight of many advisors and investors.

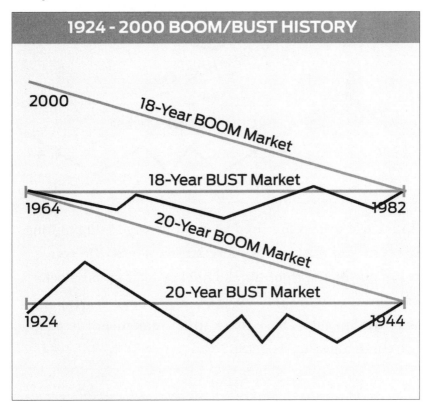

The year 2000 was marked by the technology bubble burst that kicked off another uncannily timed bear market. This lost decade of growth was further propelled by the mortgage collapse in 2008 (see graph on the following page).

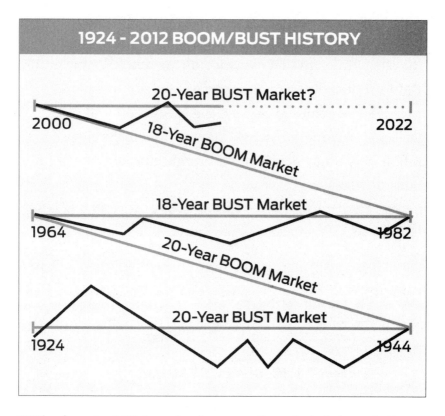

With close to 100 hundred years of market data pointing to boom and bust cycles every 20 years or so, do you think now is the right time to hold or load up on stocks and funds? Before you answer that, remember what Santayana said: "Those that cannot remember the past are condemned to repeat it."

> **Maybe it's time to stop the insanity.**
> **Maybe it's time to rescue your retirement**
> **from a secular bear market.**
> **As Ronald Reagan once said, "Facts**
> **are stubborn things."**

Maybe it's time to stop the insanity. Maybe it's time to rescue your retirement from a secular bear market. As Ronald Reagan once said, "Facts are stubborn things."

THE THREE BIGGEST THREATS TO YOUR WEALTH

Threat to Wealth #1
MONEY

Everyone likes talking about money. Admit it. Making money, saving money, spending money, complaining about money, investing money, etc. Heck, turn on any news station for 10 minutes and I bet there will be at least one story dealing with money.

Because of the highly publicized stories of Bernie Madoff, Enron, and about every politician, money has been associated with greed. But, I ask, "Can't money be used for good?"

Money is just a tool. You can use that tool poorly or prudently. I've had some tremendously positive experiences using the money I've worked hard for and been blessed with. I've been to Honduras for missions, helped sustain an orphanage for children with HIV/AIDs, supported local performing arts, and even sent a couple on a cruise to enjoy their last months together (he had terminal cancer).

I'm not trying to turn this into a conversation on the social values of money, but rather its significance in our lives. (Try living without it and see how far you get.) After all, money is simply the oil that lubricates the economic engine. Lubricant that greases the wheels of an economy.

MONEY MAKES THE ECONOMY GO AROUND

Money is the lubricant that greases the wheels of an economy. I want you to close your eyes and focus on this for a minute: Picture a big engine. Imagine all the gears, all interconnected, working in harmony. It's grimy, it's dirty, it's steamy, and it's noisy in there.

Got the image in your mind?

Now, imagine we flush all the grease out of the engine. What happens? You hear the gears grinding to a screeching halt like nails on a chalkboard. To fix the problem you flood the engine with grease so thick you can't even see the gears. What happens now? The gears overheat from the friction, springs start popping out all over, and all heck breaks loose.

What's the moral of the story?

While grease is critical to the smooth operation of the engine, if you supply too little or too much, you can really foul things up. The same applies to money in an economy. While money is the lubricant that greases the wheels of an economy, too little or too much can really foul things up. This example applies to our first big threat to your hard-earned retirement savings: the supply of money.

"M3" is what economists call the measure of money supply. Man, that's creative. (See why I was not overly interested with this stuff in college?) Hopefully, you found my engine analogy a lot more interesting. Anyway, M3 is simple in the fact that it measures the supply of money in a given economy. The problem I've discovered is the long-lasting effects of having too little/too much money supply in the economy.

ROBERT'S RULE

While money is the lubricant that greases the wheels of an economy, too little or too much can really foul things up.

It's largely the Federal Reserve's responsibility to monitor, print, inject and retract the supply of money in the economy. You may be wondering why the Fed would inject/retract money in the economy. There are several reasons why they would choose one or the other, but I don't want to get enmeshed in that discussion.

Let's focus on the big picture. What happens if there's an oversupply of money in an economy? This is what can hit you where it counts – your wallet – especially in retirement.

Think of it this way. Pull out your wallet or purse. Yes, I'm serious. Pull out a $20 bill and look at it carefully. (If you spent your last $20 to buy this book, that was a wise investment, but still play along.)

Do you know what you're holding in your hand?

I know, I know, $20. But really, do you know what you're holding?

What you have in your hot little hand is 20 "shares" of the United States of America. Let that sink in for a couple of minutes.

OK, now let's say you own 20 shares of Microsoft stock and the company decides to "print" more shares of stock. What effect does this have on your existing 20 shares? The answer is, your share value becomes diluted. They're worth less now.

> **With ever-increasing longevity, many retirees are living 30 years or more into their golden years. If inflation averages 3%, then every 10 years your money loses 30% of its purchasing power. This is a real problem if you wish to maintain your lifestyle.**

How is this different than when the government "prints" more money, or "shares" of the United States? Does it dilute your existing "shares?" Sure it does. It dilutes your 20 "shares" of the United States, and they eventually become worthless.

The end result? Classic inflation, the loss of purchasing power over time. Your "shares" buy fewer and fewer goods. Long-term increased money supply in turn creates inflation, which in turn creates a devastating environment for retirees.

It's safe to assume that you'll live a long and vibrant retirement. With ever-increasing longevity, many retirees are living 30 years or more into their golden years. If inflation averages 3%, then every 10 years your money loses 30% of its purchasing power. This is a real problem if you wish to maintain your lifestyle. After all, isn't that one of your main goals for retirement – maintaining your lifestyle? This very real threat of inflation, of course, is all compounded by the "easy money" policy of the Federal Reserve and U.S. government.

GOOD AS GOLD?

By many estimates, the U.S. dollar has already fallen in value by 98% when compared to gold (since President Nixon took the United States off the gold standard in 1971). The Federal Reserve has increased the money supply by so much and manipulated interest rates to such low levels that investors have been forced into risky investments at quite possibly the worst time. The proof is at your bank. Go to the nearest bank and ask for its current savings and CD rates.

With unprecedented bailout programs and an unchecked federal spending spree, it's safe to say that the money supply is at very high levels. In other words, the government has "printed" massive amounts of money and taken on massive amounts of debt, pushing the supply of money to extreme levels and quite possibly setting the stage for high inflation in the near future. This is an attack (albeit possibly unintended) on the current and future generations of retirees.

INFLATION ON STEROIDS

The poster child for out-of-control inflation is the recent example of Zimbabwe, where the supply of money far outweighed the demand, forcing hyperinflation to take hold at a 98% daily inflation rate. That meant that it only took about a day for goods to double in price. While this is an extreme example of inflation caused by "easy money" policies, it certainly paints the picture of the severe effects it can have on your retirement.

No one knows for sure how harsh inflation will be in the United States over the next 10 to 20 years, but one thing is for sure: It's up to you to take action and protect your hard-earned retirement income.

SHORT-TERM THINKING, LONG-TERM IMPACT

The long-term impact of the Fed's "easy money" policy:

- Inflation, specifically higher commodity prices such as oil, cotton, wheat, metals, etc.
- The U.S. dollar will be worth less and buy less.
- Conservative savers will be penalized because they will earn less on their "safe money" due to low interest rates.
- Many stocks will buckle under the pressure of higher commodity prices and cash-strapped consumers buying fewer goods.

All in all, the United States will feel the crushing debt load and will eventually succumb to severe austerity measures as recently witnessed in Greece, Italy, Portugal and Spain.

This is a difficult environment to invest in because many stocks will do poorly, while the safe harbor of bonds will drastically diminish.

BOND INVESTORS' WORST NIGHTMARE

Bond and bond fund investors will fall victim when the Fed ultimately raises interest rates to combat the excess money supply. Mid- to long-term duration bonds/bond funds will be the most devastated. For example, an increase in interest rates of only 1% will cause longer term bonds to lose 15% or more – a 15% loss in what's considered a "safe" investment!

Sound depressing? Fear not, an answer for rescuing your retirement in this high money supply environment can be found later in this book. The important thing to take away from this discussion is that you need to have a plan to rescue your retirement from the devastating effects of inflation. Since I've armed you with the knowledge of M3, let's discover the next biggest threat to your retirement.

Threat to Wealth #2
RETIREMENT INCOME THE WRONG WAY

What does your ideal retirement look like? Paint that picture in your mind. Imagine yourself enjoying the absolute perfect retirement, designed by YOU.

Are you traveling? Spending time with your grandkids? Playing golf every day? Volunteering? Or simply having the freedom to choose what you want to do?

Now imagine running out of money.

How do you feel? What does that do to your ideal retirement lifestyle?

Will you have to get a job? Or worse, move in with the kids? Gasp!

Running out of money is a real threat to retirees and aspiring retirees. According to recent polling, it's the number one concern to those entering retirement[3].

> **Running out of money is a real threat to retirees and aspiring retirees. According to recent polling, it's the number one concern to those entering retirement.**

For a real-life cautionary tale, look to the American Airlines pension default in 2012, the largest default in American history, affecting 130,000 employees:

> *"A bankrupt company will do anything it can to cut costs, so it's no surprise American [Airlines] wants to dump their pension plans."*
> – Josh Gotbaum, Director, PBGC

American Airline's plan was taken over by the PBGC (Pension Benefit Guaranty Corporation), as were the plans of GM, Delphi, Circuit City, Delta Pilots, Lehman Brothers, Polaroid, United Airlines and US Airways, among many, many others.

According to Reuters, "The PBGC is owned by the government, but it's funded through insurance premiums paid by plan sponsors. The PBGC has a long-term $26 billion deficit due to an unprecedented run of plan failures during the recession, but it has plenty of cash to meet near-term obligations."

How safe is your pension?

No one knows for absolute sure, but according to a recent front page article in *USA Today*, it may be worse than once thought for federal retirees:

> *"Retirement programs for former federal workers – civilian and military – are growing so fast they now face a multi-trillion-dollar shortfall nearly as big as Social Security's."*
>
> – *USA Today*, Sept. 2011

The recurring theme is that you may have been promised a private or public pension, but don't count on it as a guaranteed promise. In the end, the only person you can count on is the person you see in the mirror every morning. It's up to you to have saved enough money for retirement.

But saving enough for retirement is only half the battle. Crazy as it sounds, that's the easy part. The real

> **Saving enough for retirement is only half the battle. Crazy as it sounds, that's the easy part. The real battle is turning your life savings into retirement income you can't outlive. How are you going to guarantee income from your investments?**

battle is turning your life savings into retirement income that you can't outlive.

How are you going to guarantee income from your investments?

TAKING INCOME FROM GROWTH ASSETS

Are you planning for your stock or mutual fund portfolio to pave the way for years of retirement income? Don't be so sure.

Dr. David Babble, professor of risk management at the Wharton School of Business warns:

> *"If you have a stock portfolio and you withdraw*
> *4% per year + inflation...you have a 90% chance of*
> *running out of money in retirement [over 30 years]."*
> *– Marketplace, May 2011*

The doctor of risk management says that you have a 90% chance of running out of money in retirement with your stock portfolio! I know, I know, your broker/advisor told you that you can withdraw 3% to 4% per year and you shouldn't run out of money. If he or she is confident that you won't run out of money, ask them this question: "If I run out of money can I move in with you and your family?"

Don't want to move in with your advisor or your kids? Then move your money to an advisor who truly specializes in income planning.

What Dr. Babble was referring to is a form of dollar cost averaging, or DCA. You've probably heard of DCA – investing equal amounts into the stock market to smooth out the volatility over time. DCA has an evil twin brother you've probably never met: RDCA (reverse dollar cost averaging), a concept that is foreign to many retirees and even their advisors.

ROBERT'S RULE

Don't want to move in with your advisor or
your kids? Then move your money to an
advisor who truly specializes in
income planning.

REVERSE DOLLAR COST AVERAGING (RDCA)

The negative effect of RDCA revolves around the impact
of taking income from investments during a volatile cycle.
It's really all about the compounding effect of losses, with-
drawals and fees. RDCA can kill your retirement because
of four factors:

- Losing money in the market
- Taking money out to meet living expenses
- Paying investment fees
- Loss of purchasing power (inflation)

Consider the chart on the following page from Rydex that
shows the history of the Dow Jones over the last 100 or
so years.

Many brokers and advisors will tell you that over
the "long term" (10 to 15 years), the market will go up.
Consider the period from 1906 to 1924 (the first bear
market in the chart). If you held stocks during this long
period you would have lost more than 4% of your money.
A loss of only 4% might not seem that devastating – after
all, there have certainly been worse times in the market.

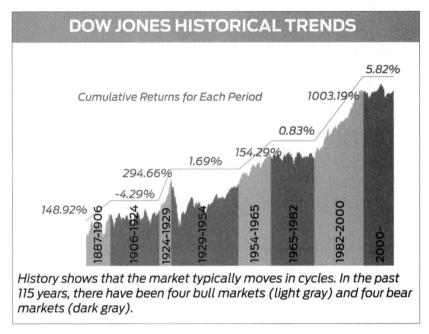

DOW JONES HISTORICAL TRENDS

5.82%

Cumulative Returns for Each Period   1003.19%

0.83%

154.29%

1.69%

294.66%

-4.29%

148.92%

1887-1906
1906-1924
1924-1929
1929-1954
1954-1965
1965-1982
1982-2000
2000-

History shows that the market typically moves in cycles. In the past 115 years, there have been four bull markets (light gray) and four bear markets (dark gray).

What else happened during those 18 years? Inflation. If inflation averaged about 3% per year, you would have lost 54% of your spending power. Add this to the market losses, and your total loss becomes 58% during this 18-year period that you remained faithful to the market.

HOW TO RUN OUT OF MONEY WITH $1 MILLION

Let's assume that you had a $1 million nest egg back in 1906 and you needed income of $36,000 per year. Over 18 years you would have depleted your account by $648,000, and your balance would be $352,000. When you factor in an average inflation rate of 3% (many believe inflation will be much higher in the future), your money would buy 54% less goods as described above.

So, while your stock account balance shows $352,000, your real purchasing power is $161,920 in inflation-adjusted dollars. And this doesn't include investment fees! In about 28 more months you could be flat broke.

What will you do for income over the next 18 years?

A MORE RECENT EXAMPLE

You may be saying, Rob, this is based on data from 1906, and now there are more controls in place. I like your critical thinking, so here's a recent example showing the effects of RDCA on your $1 million in the most recent decade.

The Devastating Effect of RDCA in Recent Years	
Date	**$1 Million - Fees - Income RMD**
1/1/2000	$1,000,000
1/1/2001	$944,385
1/1/2002	$815,533
1/1/2003	$626,662
1/1/2004	$771,229
1/1/2005	$727,814
1/1/2006	$710,033
1/1/2007	$775,469
1/1/2008	$729,386
1/1/2009	$431,950
1/1/2010	$507,848
12/1/2010	$529,307 balance after 10 years

There's the cold, hard truth about taking income the wrong way. Over the last decade, your $1 million is basically cut in half.

What you're witnessing is the awesome effect of compounding working against you, slowly eroding your ideal retirement. As you continue to take income, you further compound any losses and fees because you are taking a larger and larger percentage out every year.

It's as simple as this: If you needed $30,000 a year to live on, you would need to withdraw 3% on $1 million. But 10 years later that same $30,000 requires you to

ROBERT'S RULE

Your income shouldn't depend on the
markets; it should depend on math.

withdraw 5.7% of your account. This snowball effect ravages your retirement savings and robs you of the peace of mind you crave.

Could the market come roaring back? Sure. But understand one simple thing: You have no control of whether the market goes up or down. No one does. Remember what you learned in the beginning of this chapter – we are in the middle of a secular bear market.

Your income shouldn't depend on the markets; it should depend on math.

In an effort to provide a fair and balanced book, let's say I'm wrong about this bear market thing (I admit it, I can't control the market either!), and the market comes roaring back. Let's say you make 10% the next few years, followed by one down year. Let's examine how RDCA continues to affect your money.

A Much-Needed Dose of Reality		
Year	Assumed Growth	Growth of $529,307 - Fees - Income RMD
11	+10%	$543,504
12	+10%	$558,886
13	+10%	$575,552
14	(10%)	$487,996 balance

Not bad performance, considering your money made 10% for three years straight and then only lost 10%. I imagine a lot of people would be OK with these returns overall. But look at how your $1 million is only worth $487,996 after a 30% run-up in the markets!

BUT WAIT, THERE'S MORE

I've left something out of the previous two charts. Since you're smarter than the average bear, I bet you can guess what it is.

Inflation.

Over time, inflation tends to average about 3% per year, so over the last 14 years, your money buys 42% less. Your $1 million is worth $487,996 and buys 42% less food, gas and services. Your $487,996 really only has the purchasing power of $283,037.

Don't forget that you'll need income for the next 10 to 15 years (or more).

How secure would you feel if this was your IRA or retirement savings? Would you have to change your lifestyle? Would you have to travel less? Get a job? Cut back on going out to eat? Move to a new neighborhood? Spoil the grandkids less?

This is the point in the book where I have to take

> **You need to do everything in your power to guarantee you will not outlive your life savings in retirement. Can you be courageous enough to stand up and take control of your financial future? Or are you going to stand idly by and let a broker or advisor tell you that you shouldn't run out of money based on some computer simulations?**

off my author's hat and put on my stern, but loving, parent's hat.

You need to do everything in your power to guarantee you will not outlive your life savings in retirement. Can you be courageous enough to stand up and take control of your financial future? Or are you going to stand idly by and let a broker or advisor tell you that you shouldn't run out of money based on some computer simulations?

Let me say one more time: Your income shouldn't depend on the markets; it should depend on math. And the math tells you that RDCA during volatile markets could cause you to run out of money before running out of breath. Over the last 10 years you would be well on your way to running out of money in retirement.

Make your mind up right now to go on a hunt for an advice-giver that specializes in creating guaranteed income plans.

Threat to Wealth #3
THE NEXT BIG BUBBLE

One of the most significant market bubbles in world history wasn't in stocks, real estate, currencies or credit. It was in tulips. That's right, flowers.

In 1636 a mass hysteria surrounding tulips overcame the Dutch as investors traded tulips in stock exchanges with prices determined by scarcity and

prestige. Economists pinpoint this event as the world's first economic bubble.

How serious was this tulip craze? At its height, tulip investors offered 12 acres of prime land for one single Viceroy bulb. All this for a flower that blooms in April and May for about a week!

The tulip obsession swept through Europe, not unlike the tech bubble of 2000 or the real estate bubble of 2008. Even the French were overcome with tulip hysteria – in some cases, people paid upward of 10 times their annual

> **Paying 10 times your annual salary for a tulip bulb seems downright insane. But I'm sure at the time it seemed perfectly rational for tulips to fetch such outrageous prices. It's only through the lens of history that everything becomes clear.**

salaries to purchase just one tulip bulb. A bulb could easily be worth more than the house it was planted in front of.

The Semper Augustus variety is famous for being the most expensive tulip during the craze. Beautiful, but is it worth 10 times your annual salary?

SEEMS CRAZY, HUH?

Paying 10 times your annual salary for a tulip bulb seems downright insane. But I'm sure at the time it seemed perfectly rational for tulips to fetch such outrageous prices. It's only through the lens of history that everything becomes clear. The same lens could be applied to real estate investors in Florida, Arizona or California in 2007. Now, of course, it seems crazy that ordinary people were being approved for sub-prime mortgages worth many times their annual salaries so they could flip real estate.

The same is true of stock market investors during the 1990s putting money in technology stocks that never posted profits, let alone revenues, from operations. One classic example of this perfectly acceptable hysteria comes from C/NET.com:

> *"Take online pet-supply store Pets.com. Its talking sock puppet mascot became so popular that it appeared in a multimillion-dollar Super Bowl commercial and as a balloon in the Macy's Thanksgiving Day parade. But as cute – or possibly annoying – as the sock puppet was, Pets.com was never able to give pet owners a compelling reason to buy supplies online. After they ordered kitty litter, a customer had to wait a few days to actually get it. And let's face it, when you need kitty litter, you need kitty litter. Moreover, because the company had to undercharge for shipping costs to attract customers, it actually lost money on most of the items it sold. The Amazon.com-backed Pets.com raised $82.5 million in an IPO in February 2000 before collapsing nine months later."*

Even the sharpest minds in the business were susceptible to the dot-com craze. Disney felt the sting of the bubble with their Go.com venture:

> *"Disney was never able to make Go.com popular enough to validate the millions spent on promotion. In Jan. 2001, Go.com was shut down, and Disney took a write-off of $790 million."*

While these bubbles seem insane looking back, they seemed perfectly rational at the time. Ditto for the world's next big bubble.

TULIPS, STOCKS AND REAL ESTATE WERE CHILD'S PLAY

What's worse than the tulip, stock and real estate bubbles? The next big bubble, which may very well make the last few bubbles look like child's play. In fact, this bubble has been brewing and festering for over 30 long

> **I think it's safe to assume that if you had a "do over" you would avoid the last few bubbles. But what if you could potentially avoid the next big bubble? Would you have the courage to take action to protect your wealth?**

years. It's so big, the majority of the world's wealth is invested in this one asset class. Globally, this gigantic bubble is $95 trillion in size. Compare that to $55 trillion globally in stocks and about $10 trillion in savings and money markets[4].

You may be wondering why so many people have invested so much money in this potentially deadly asset class. It's simply because it appears perfectly rational for you to put your money in this investment, just like investing in tulips in 1636, buying real estate in 2007, or buying tech stocks in 1999.

I think it's safe to assume that if you had a "do over" you would avoid the last few bubbles. But what if you could potentially avoid the next big bubble? Would you have the courage to take action to protect your wealth?

I'm exposing this next bubble for you ahead of time so you can act now and protect your life savings. And I'm sounding the warning bell with some credibility. Many years ago, I authored a weekly column for several newspapers in Ohio. In one particular column I warned readers of an impending recession and market crash:

> *"It blows me away that the broad-based financial media and the major brokerage firms are still quick to tell investors that it's time to buy in the market, but is it? You know, it's real easy to tell someone else to risk THEIR money, especially when they're paid to tell you that."*

I continued:

> *"The mortgage and residential real estate market continues to play a negative role in the U.S. stock market as home foreclosures continue to set new records. Couple that with an inverted yield curve, continued terrorist threats, uncertainty in Iraq, and the U.S. dollar being the lowest value since 1971 – and you've got a nice recipe for a recession and a stock market crash."*

Did your advisor or whoever you trust for advice warn you about the market crash ahead of time?

"Some would accuse me of being pessimistic, but I would counter that I'm being realistic...that I'm not buying into the boloney that the major brokerage firms are pushing..."

I concluded my article with a dire call to action:

"...I personally believe that, if you're retired or close to retirement, there's never been a better time to play it safe with your life savings. With all these signs pointing to another possible market downturn, why would you want to risk losing a large amount of your life savings again? It's all about your peace of mind at this point."

I wrote this article Sept. 15, 2007 – within 30 days of the all-time stock market high! What if you had heard my warning back in 2007 and taken some chips off the table? Would you have avoided some stress in your financial life? Would you have more money now and a more positive outlook for your retirement? Could you retire earlier?

I ask you this because I firmly believe that you should heed my next bubble warning and take corrective action now in order to protect your life savings.

DEVASTATED DREAMS

I believe this next big bubble will destroy more wealth and devastate more dreams than the previous bubble crashes. I believe that in the aftermath of this crash, investors and media pundits will look back through the lens of history and reflect how insane it was to put so

much money into this investment at such high prices –
kind of like tulip bulbs.

What's really remarkable is the perceived safety of this
investment. In fact, most investors buy this investment for
that very reason, safety. And in such an uncertain world I
don't blame them.

After all, safety of principal is the new sexy.

Unfortunately, in this next bubble trap, safety is the
cheese and you're the mouse. In fact, at one point, I too
was a devout mouse. I was susceptible until I understood
the writing on the wall: that this bubble was growing to
such a magnitude that it would inevitably explode. I knew
I must do something to protect my clients' wealth NOW.

My purpose in warning you, dear reader, is to
sincerely help you preserve your irreplaceable savings,
just like I warned market participants back in 2007.

THE NEXT BIG BUBBLE IS...

Sophisticated real estate investors understand the proper
use of debt and how it can juice up your investment when
used prudently. Small business owners also understand
the appropriate use of debt: to grow business, buy out
competitors, innovate and expand operations. Those in
the know understand the correct use of debt. Everyone
else is investing in bad debt.

The next big bubble is built on a mountain of bad
debt $95 trillion dollars high. I call it bad debt, because
I believe it will explode and annihilate trillions of dollars
in wealth around the globe. This bad debt that has

created the next bubble is in fixed income. Fixed income, or bonds, appear to be safe, but once you pull back the covers you see the naked truth.

THE NAKED TRUTH

Bonds have had such a wild 30+ year run that investors have piled their savings into them at precisely the wrong time. The crux of this bubble is so simple, so easy to comprehend, you can grasp it with a grade-school metaphor,

ROBERT'S RULE

When the "heavy" kid gets off the seesaw, the skinny kid crashes to the ground. In other words, when interest rates rise (even a nominal amount), bond prices fall.

the seesaw. Do you remember playing on the seesaw at school? If you were like me, you never wanted to share the seesaw with the "heavy" kid in class because you would skyrocket in the air when he got on.

If you can understand how a seesaw works, then you'll understand why bonds are the next bubble. On the bond seesaw, you have interest rates on one end and bond prices on the other end.

It doesn't take a rocket scientist to figure out where interest rates are right now. Just take a look at your checking account, savings account, CD or money market account. Your money is earning pretty darn near zero interest. So, the skinny kid is bond prices, which have skyrocketed.

INTEREST RATES ARE THE "HEAVY" KID

Pretty simple, huh? Interest rates are at historic lows, so bond prices are at historic highs. I believe that if you're holding or buying bonds or bond funds at this point in time, you're buying at such an extreme high it could be like buying tulips, tech stocks or real estate at their bubble highs.

WHAT HAPPENS WHEN RATES RISE?

When the "heavy" kid gets off the seesaw, the skinny kid crashes to the ground. In other words, when interest rates rise (even a nominal amount), bond prices fall. The relationship between rates and bond prices can be pretty dramatic at the current sky-high levels.

HOW MUCH WILL IT TAKE TO START THE NEXT CRASH?

We all want to make more interest at the bank. Savers are being punished by low yields, and a 1% interest rate doesn't put food on the table or come close to keeping up with inflation. It's perfectly natural to want a better return on your money, but when – notice I didn't say "if" – interest rates go up, I believe it will wipe out a lot of wealth around the world.

It will only take a small rise in interest rates to pop the bond bubble. Only a diminutive increase of 1% in

> **It will only take a small rise in interest rates to pop the bond bubble. Only a diminutive increase of 1% in interest rates will cause a steep drop in prices by 15% or more, depending on bond maturity lengths.**

interest rates will cause a steep drop in prices by 15% or more, depending on bond maturity lengths. Generally speaking, the longer the bond term, the greater the volatility to interest rates. Furthermore, the greater the rise in interest rates, the greater the loss.

It's unmistakable that bond prices have an inverse relationship to interest rates. Fixed income investments (bonds) can be hazardous to your financial health when interest rates are low, because the interest they earn is fixed. Having a fixed interest rate is beneficial when rates are high. Again, the problem right now is that interest rates are at historic lows, and like tax rates, there's really only one direction that they can go – up!

Have you or someone you know refinanced a mortgage in the last few years? That was a smart move because rates are so low right now. What if the going mortgage rate was 9%? Would you refinance your 5% loan to a 9% loan? Of course not, for the very same reason I'm advocating that you steer clear of bonds, especially mid- to long-term maturities.

Why would anyone want to invest in bonds and bond funds right now, when rates are so low and bond prices are at a 30+ year high? The secret recipe to investing in anything is to buy low and sell high, right?

> *Bond real returns are "at a historic high, 96.1% above the predicted trend." The last time bonds were this high was "in 1940, 86% above the trend." That was at the tail end of the Great Depression when investors distrusted stocks and piled into bonds. "Today bond prices are already above that point."*
>
> *– MarketWatch.com, Oct. 2011*

The point MarketWatch was making is that the bond market is at an all-time high. They didn't say a 10-year

> **Why would anyone want to invest in bonds and bond funds right now, when rates are so low and bond prices are at a 30+ year high? The secret recipe to investing in anything is buy low and sell high, right?**

high; they said the highest EVER in history. Shouldn't bond owners be selling right now at the all-time high?

One of the greatest gifts from our Creator is the power of choice. I don't know about you, but I hate situations where my choices have been limited, or worse, forced on me. As soon as interest rates rise, you're stuck. Your only choice is to hold the bond to maturity to get your money back, or sell at a loss.

To my surprise, even the world's largest bond manager, Bill Gross, founder of PIMCO funds, echoes my bond bubble fears:

> *"Unless a hundred years of financial history are meaningless, bonds must go down – and yields and interest rates, up."*
>
> *– MarketWatch.com, Oct. 2011*

As you can see below, the calculation of the dollar loss impact of rising interest rates is pretty straightforward:

$$B(0,t)$$

$$= E\left[\exp\left(-\int_0^t r_s\,ds\right)\Big|r_0\right] = E\left[e^{-R_t}\,|\,r_0\right]$$

$$= \exp\left[-\left\{\frac{2\{1-\exp(-\sqrt{a^2+2\sigma^2}t)\}}{\left[\begin{array}{l}\{(\sqrt{a^2+2\sigma^2}+a)\\ +(\sqrt{a^2+2\sigma^2}-a)\exp(\sqrt{a^2+2\sigma^2}t)\}\end{array}\right]}\right\}r_0\right]$$

$$\times\left\{\frac{2\sqrt{a^2+2\sigma^2}\exp\{-[(\sqrt{a^2+2\sigma^2}-a)/2]t\}}{\left[\begin{array}{l}(\sqrt{a^2+2\sigma^2}+a)\\ +(\sqrt{a^2+2\sigma^2}-a)\exp(\sqrt{a^2+2\sigma^2}t)\end{array}\right]}\right\}^{2b/\sigma^2},$$

I'm joking, but if you can figure out that formula you should help me write the sequel to this book!

I prefer to keep things a tad simpler. Say you own a $100,000 bond or a bond fund paying 5% interest, which pays you $5,000 per year. If interest rates rise by only 1%

and new bond issues are earning 6% interest, it can negatively affect the price of your bond. Why? Because no one wants to buy your bond that pays $5,000 in interest when they can buy a "new" bond that pays $6,000 in interest. Got it? If you want or need to sell your bond to keep up with inflation or to support your lifestyle, then you'll have to sell it at a loss.

SEQUENCE OF EVENTS LEADING TO BOND LOSSES (OVERSIMPLIFIED)

- You own a $100,000 ABC bond paying 5%, or $5,000 a year.
- Interest rates rise 1%, thereby increasing new bond yields.
- New XYZ bonds pay 6%, or $6,000 a year.
- Sell your ABC bond at a 17% loss. Approximate bond value is $83,334, because at this price it will yield the same as the going rate on XYZ bonds, or $6,000 a year.

Isn't that a lot easier to understand than the preceding mathematical formula? The formula is far more precise, but you get the gist, and that's what counts.

THE TOP CRITICISMS OF MY BUBBLE THESIS

Like other "Paul Reveres" of our time, I am not without my critics (just like when I made my call in 2007). On the next two pages are the most commonly expressed criticisms and objections to my thoughts on the next big bubble. My desire is to arm you with the facts.

"Interest rates won't rise anytime soon"

Maybe. The Federal Reserve has stated that it plans to keep (manipulate) rates low in the short term. Honestly, can you trust anything that comes out of Washington? Furthermore, interest rates can rise due to poor bond auctions like they did in Spain, Greece, Italy, Ireland and Portugal, because of distrust of those governments to be fiscally responsible. Sound familiar? I still wonder with rates so low and bond prices so high, why anyone would want to be holding bonds right now, anyway?

"When interest rates rise, we will get out of bonds."

Timing is everything. The question is, can you or anyone time this, or are you playing with fire? Not to step on toes, but what was your experience with timing the market in 2008? I can tell you from experience that no one can time any market. I was good (and, frankly, lucky in some respects) in 2007 to call the all-time high of the market within 30 days. Know your limits and you will be truly wise.

"Rising interest rates will only affect long-term bonds"

Long-term bonds are certainly the riskiest bonds, but short and intermediate length maturities are certainly not immune to rising interest rates. Many remember Oct. 19, 1987 as "Black Monday" because of how much they lost in the stock market. However, many are surprised to learn that far more wealth in terms of dollar value was lost in bonds on "Black Monday" than in stocks. Why? Because interest rates rose from 7.29% to 10.25%, causing bond prices of varying maturities to plunge just like my seesaw example earlier.

"Own bond funds because they're professionally managed."

Bond funds are inferior to owning individual bonds, because you have zero control from the get-go. You're at the mercy of the fund manager to navigate a bond portfolio that will lose ground rapidly when rates rise.

Bond funds are inferior to owning individual bonds, because you have zero control from the get-go. You're at the mercy of the fund manager to navigate a bond portfolio that will lose ground rapidly when rates rise.

Understand that the mandate of fixed income funds is to be invested in bonds, not to sell and hold cash. I don't think bond fund managers will be able to avoid this bubble, just like virtually all of the stock fund managers were unable to avoid the crash of 2008.

BONUS FACTS FOR BOND OWNERS

While rising interest rates are certainly the deadliest foe to bonds right now, they aren't the only risk bond investors should be aware of. Turn the page for more information on bond risks.

Bond Risks You Need to Know About

Risk	Outcome
Interest Rates	As rates rise, bond prices fall.
Default	Bond issuer fails to make interest payments.
Prepayment	Bond issuer "calls" bond back before maturity.
Reinvestment	A "called" bond is reinvested at a lower rate.
Market	Overall market declines, affecting individual bonds with otherwise strong fundamentals.
Stock Market	Stock market declines and redemptions affect bond funds because they are trading on the stock market.
Liquidity	Selling at a loss because the bond is meeting weak demand.
Inflation	Higher than expected future inflation erodes the value of principal and interest payments.

CRITICAL QUESTIONS YOU MUST ASK YOURSELF BEFORE CONTINUING

Do you feel that inflation is a real threat? If so, how has your advisor protected you?

Do you worry about running out of money in retirement? Do you have a plan that protects your income and your lifestyle?

Do you own bonds or bond funds right now at the all-time high? Why? What are you hoping to achieve? Are you interested in learning alternative strategies[5] to lessen volatility and provide a good yield?

KNOWLEDGE IS POWER

They say that knowledge is power. That's wrong. Knowledge is *potential* power. It's what you do with the

> **They say that knowledge is power. That's wrong. Knowledge is *potential* power. It's what you do with the knowledge that creates real power.**

knowledge that creates real power. I've entrusted you with my once-secret economic arbitrage tools, previously only available to my clients and business partners.

Remember, dear reader, with great knowledge comes great responsibility. Use it wisely to protect your hard-earned money and discover new opportunities for creating additional wealth!

LET NOT YOUR HEART BE TROUBLED

I imagine this part of the book may have been a little discouraging, even downright depressing. Good, then I got through to you.

My intent is not for you to read this chapter and then call your doctor to request a prescription for Prozac. No, my intent is to shock you with the truth and hard facts, even move you off center a bit. Because only then will you truly take action to rescue your retirement from bad advice and protect your irreplaceable savings and investments from inflation, reverse dollar cost averaging and the next big bubble crash.

With these dire events lying in wait to hold your retirement hostage, I want you to know that there's hope. There's a solution to every problem. The three biggest threats to your wealth can be avoided, but it requires action, an open mind and courage on your part.

Read on to discover my strategies to rescuing your retirement and putting you firmly back in control of your financial future.

Chapter 4
INVESTMENT SECRETS OF THE ULTRA-WEALTHY

or

BILLIONAIRE INVESTING FOR THE MILLIONAIRE NEXT DOOR

"Wall Street is the only place people ride to in a Rolls-Royce to get advice from those who took the subway."

– Warren Buffett

CAUTION!

This is a difficult subject to tackle in a book. After all, I'm about to dismantle almost everything you've been taught about investing.

If you still want to continue to use the investment strategies for those who are less wealthy, then by all means knock yourself out. But read on if you want to learn about the investment strategies of the ultra-wealthy.

All I ask is that you approach this chapter with an open mind.

"Real knowledge is to know the extent of one's ignorance."

– Confucius

Realize that you don't know what you don't know. Let me give you an example by asking you two simple questions. The only thing I ask is that you answer them out loud. I know, I know, your spouse or the person next to you on the plane may look at you funny, but do it anyway. It'll be fun.

Question 1
What two colors make up a STOP sign?
Answer
Red and white, right?

Question 2
What two colors make up a YIELD sign?
Answer
Yellow and black, right?

Pretty simple questions, right? But are you sure of your answers? Are stop signs really red and white, and yield signs really yellow and black?

Well, one out of two isn't bad.

What? Stop signs are, in fact, red and white. But you got the yield sign question wrong.

> **Using Einstein's definition of insanity, one could conclude that it's totally insane to invest the same way you always have and expect different results.**

Yield signs haven't been yellow and black since the 1980s! Yield signs are red and white. OK, pick your chin up off the table.

What does this simple, but profound, exercise teach you (other than the fact that yield signs haven't been yellow and black for about 30 years)?

It's that the world has changed around you, but you're still operating in the old "normal." I bet you're investing that way, too. Do I have your attention now?

Remember what Einstein said about insanity? It's "doing the same thing over and over again and expecting a different result." Using Einstein's definition of insanity, one could conclude that it's totally insane to invest the same way you always have and expect different results. In fact, I believe that your investment tools and strategies should change and evolve over time based on innovation and your stage of life.

Honestly, have you been happy with the results of your investments over the last 10 to 12 years? Can you be honest enough to admit that you've invested in the same manner as you always have, but expected a different

> **The last decade of the stock market can certainly be described as insane. It's not because stocks are bad investments. It's because you've been told to invest the same way over and over again and expect different results.**

result? Now, the million-dollar question is: Are you fed up enough to actually do something about it?

The last decade of the stock market can certainly be described as insane. It's not because stocks are bad investments. It's because you've been told to invest the same way over and over again and expect different results.

ARE YOU READY TO STOP THE INSANITY?

I'm not trying to insult you, my dear reader and purchaser of this fine book. But when I reflect on my experience of working with the ultra-wealthy, there's one thing that stands out in my mind above all else: You're not doing what they're doing. Again, I'm not trying to offend you, but they're doing different things differently. I'm not saying it because you don't run a Fortune 500 company or fly around in a private jet. What I mean is that your approach to investing is significantly different than theirs. They've stopped the insanity!

You're being told to invest like yield signs are yellow and black, but now you know they're not. Why is it, do you think, that during the last market crash the ultra-wealthy stayed ultra-wealthy? It's because they invest differently than you do. Do they own stocks and bonds? Sure, to a relatively small degree. More importantly, they use some strategies and investments that you've never heard of, let alone use. Why? Well, the truth(s) may shock you.

Truth #1
THE GOVERNMENT

It's no secret that the government absolutely loves conformity. It's much easier to "regulate" a large number of people if they're all are doing the same thing (such as investors and their advisors, for example). If you walk like a duck and quack like a duck, then you must be a duck. A pond of ducks is a lot easier to "manage" than an entire zoo. Get the point?

With the ever-increasing government intrusion into our daily lives, you may not be surprised to know that regulators restrict your access to many investment strategies based upon the amount of wealth you've accumulated. The more wealth you have, the more investment strategies are at your disposal. The less wealth you have, the fewer investment strategies are available to you.

Government regulators restrict your access to more sophisticated strategies because they believe that more sophisticated means more complicated. I disagree. I've never met a mutual fund owner who could describe to me their fee structure or investment strategy.

I think it's safe to say that unsuccessful savers are stuck with investing the same way they always have. They're stuck with the insanity! They have to use the same old mutual funds, high-fee variable annuities and so on that have failed to provide them with any of the peace of mind they crave. And their advisors are stuck using antiquated investment strategies as well. This is why my team works exclusively with higher net worth clients – so our hands aren't tied when we're crafting a comprehensive financial strategy.

Simply put, the government manipulates the system, and unfortunately we have to play by its rules.

Truth #2
WALL STREET

Traditional financial planning and traditional investing have failed you and millions of other Americans. I believe you need a traditional financial advisor as much as you need a pediatrician. Obviously, you have no use for a pediatrician; you've matured and outgrown the need for a child's doctor. Chances are you've also outgrown your advisor, but you just haven't realized it yet.

You may be surprised, but industry insiders understand that Wall Street wants you to keep investing the "old way." On one hand, simply entrusting you with this information is going to anger a lot of people "on the street" and the advisors in your neck of the woods. On the other hand, I also feel that you cannot adequately prepare for your retirement without me blowing the lid off this closely guarded secret. It's time to wake up to different investment strategies that have been successful for the ultra-wealthy and rarely offered to those who aren't.

The hidden truth is that investment companies advise the ultra-wealthy very differently than they do you. Why? It's simple. The same reason the government restricts your access to different investment strategies: It's easier to manage a bunch of people all doing the same thing. If the clients of big-name banks and brokerage firms all have similar portfolios of stocks, bonds, mutual funds and the like, it's much, much easier to manage – all the while collecting a management fee.

This is all common knowledge to industry insiders. In fact, this hidden truth came to a head in 2012 when Lyle LaMothe, the head honcho of Merrill Lynch, resigned:

> *"...LaMothe abruptly left one of the highest profile jobs on Wall Street last May, he cited personal reasons. But in his first interview since then, LaMothe, 50, said he had "philosophical" differences with the way Bank of America Corp. approached wealth management, emphasizing the goals of the bank rather than specific needs of Merrill's brokers and clients."*
>
> – *Reuters, Feb. 2012*

Shortly thereafter, an op-ed article made its way into *The New York Times*, penned by Greg Smith, a Goldman Sachs banker, just following his resignation:

> *Smith said the bank sells financial products "that*
> *we are trying to get rid of...It makes me ill how*
> *callously people talk about ripping their clients off."*
> *– The New York Times, March 2012*

I imagine this may be a hard pill to swallow. This fact (that a lot of advisors are actually financial salesman in disguise) is something I'm sure I take for granted because I've seen the aftermath of their "advice" so many times.

I think many clients of these advisors would be discouraged if they Googled the name of their advisors' parent company and the word "fraud" (for instance, "Morgan Stanley fraud"). Here's a frighteningly recent example:

> *"Irving Picard, the trustee seeking to reclaim*
> *billions for Madoff's victims, claims Merrill Lynch*
> *International was creating and selling products*
> *tied to Madoff feeder funds even though it was*
> *aware of possible fraud within Bernard L. Madoff*
> *Investment Securities."*
> *– Forbes.com, March 2011*

Understand that you cannot change the past, but you do have the power to control your future. It is actually possible to rescue your retirement from bad advice, even at this stage in the game. You have to address how you can leverage a more sophisticated style of investing previously only available to the ultra-wealthy. If you "qualify" for special access (e.g., experienced or accredited investors with high incomes or $250,000 to $1 million in liquid assets), you, too, may be able take advantage of the investment secrets of the ultra-wealthy. Your journey of discovery begins, of all places, at the Ivy League schools of Harvard, Yale and Princeton.

> **What I found by digging through performance data were superior annualized returns by using the Ivy League alternative models compared with the average investment portfolio of 60% stocks and 40% bonds.**

IT ALL BEGAN IN THE IVY LEAGUE

The birthplace of my wealth creation and preservation strategy began with some remarkable research I discovered from Harvard, Yale and Princeton.

Imagine Einstein trying to wrap his mind around the theory of relativity. He's frantically writing formulae on a large chalkboard, working into the wee hours of the morning, knowing how close he was to making a breakthrough.

That was me – determined to discover a better, more effective way to create and preserve wealth for my clients. I knew there had to a better strategy than the old approach, and interestingly, all roads led back to the Ivy League universities and their unique investment models.

IS IT POSSIBLE TO AVERAGE 10% A YEAR?

What I found by digging through performance data were superior annualized returns using the Ivy League alternative models compared with the average investment portfolio of 60% stocks and 40% bonds. Yale's is my personal favorite model, because they have shown the most consistent performance, even during the stinky economy.

	Yale Model[5]	60/40 Portfolio	Yale's Comparison[5]
5 Years	5.5%	4.9%	>12%
10 Years	10.1%	4.3%	>135%
20 Years	14.2%	8.3%	>71%

It doesn't take a genius to figure out that over a 10-year period, a 10.1% return is stellar compared to the average investor's 4.3% return. Using basic math, a $1 million account growing at 10.1% annually would be worth nearly $1.1 million more than an account growing at 4.3% annually. Wouldn't an extra $1.1 million come in handy during retirement?

Take an even longer term view, over a 20-year period, and the math gets really interesting. If the same $1 million earns 14.2% per year, it grows to $14.2 million after 20 years. That's almost $10 million more than what an average portfolio making 8.3% per year would have made during the same 20 years. Now can you see why I was so intrigued by my research?

I certainly had enough common sense to realize that 10.1% a year is far from guaranteed, but I marveled at how the Ivy League's investment management generated consistently superior returns to the average investor's and advisor's.

I was also perplexed by how they were trumping MY returns, which I considered pretty impressive. Most importantly, how could I bring this strategy to my clients and make a positive impact on their peace of mind before and during retirement?

HOW DID THEY DO IT?

Harvard, Yale and Princeton are collectively responsible for managing more than $50 billion in investments and have earned their reputations not by chance. Because of the vast size of their portfolios, they employ a very different approach to creating and preserving wealth.

It's common knowledge that one of the best ways to achieve portfolio diversification is through asset allocation (the process of dividing investments among different kinds of asset classes). The Ivy League model takes diversification to a whole different level. What they were employing was a diversification approach unlike anything I'd ever witnessed. I dubbed it "vertical diversification" – aka the secret of the ultra-wealthy!

It seemed like such a simple concept, almost as if the answer had been right in front of me for years. Yet it required a level of expertise and sophistication that would send almost any experienced money manager into a tizzy trying to duplicate the model.

After careful examination of the inner workings of the Ivy League investment strategies (especially Yale's),

The solution I found hinged on this thing I called vertical diversification, which I defined as: asset allocation among truly non-correlated alternative investment strategies to generate an absolute return, regardless of market volatility.

I threw my hands in the air. Frustrated, I concluded these approaches were not possible for the average investor to replicate, leaving them at a severe disadvantage to their "smart money" counterparts. Because of the previously explained reasons (government and Wall Street), this strategy was secretly locked away from the majority of investors.

It wasn't until I completed considerable research, formed the right relationships and hired the right people, that I was able to replicate and possibly build upon the success of Yale's strategy.

The solution I found hinged on this thing I called vertical diversification, which I defined as: asset allocation among truly non-correlated alternative investment strategies to generate an absolute return, regardless of market volatility.

That's a lot to take in, so let me simplify it a bit.

I LIKE TO KEEP IT SIMPLE

I'm a pretty simple guy from a pretty small town in Ohio. While I work with clients from all over the world, one thing every one of them has in common is that they desire a simple plan. A plan that they can understand. Whether they have $500,000 or $50 million, they want their problems solved with a strategy they can wrap their minds around.

Because our clients come from all walks of life and investment experiences, my team and I pride ourselves in creating just the right recipe of simplicity combined with problem-solving sophistication.

While I could overwhelm you with all the details and research behind vertical diversification, I would rather explain it the way I describe it to our clients. Simply.

BUILDING YOUR FISCAL DREAM HOME

I've never physically built a house, but I know from a rudimentary level what makes up the basic structure: a roof, the walls and, of course, a foundation.

It was from this simple premise, building your dream home, that my vision of delivering the Yale model of vertical diversification to aspiring retirees and retirees was born. This quantum leap to real asset allocation turned traditional investing on its head, and explaining it proved to be difficult – until I realized it was like building a house.

Imagine you were to build your dream home today. Would you start construction on the roof or the foundation? The foundation, of course, because no matter how fancy your roof is, without a solid foundation your home will crumble to the ground.

How is that different from your investment portfolio? When constructing your ideal portfolio, shouldn't you have a solid foundation on which to build?

PREPARING THE FOUNDATION

When it comes to your money, it's mission-critical – especially in or during retirement – to have a rock-solid foundation. In terms of your fiscal dream home, I describe your foundation accounts as "safe money," which I define as money you cannot lose, unless you choose to.

While every investment or savings vehicle has some sort of risk, foundation accounts are the closest thing to risk-free as it gets. In other words, these vehicles offer some level of principal protection. Again, this is money you can't lose unless you choose to (for example, cashing it in early).

There are really only three options to choose from that meet this strict definition:

- **CDs** (backed by banks and FDIC)
- **Fixed and hybrid annuities** (backed by life insurance companies and some state insurance guaranty associations)
- **Government bonds** (backed by the government)

All three of these vehicles provide principal protection as long as you hold them to maturity. The principal protection of CDs is backed by banks and the FDIC, fixed annuities by life insurance company assets and state guaranty funds, and government bonds by the promise of the U.S. federal government.

YOU CAN'T LIVE IN THE BASEMENT FOREVER!

While the basement is certainly the keystone of your fiscal dream home, it doesn't provide much in the way of big potential returns. This is where taking some calculated risk comes in.

The "roof" of your fiscal dream home is where you're trying hit the jackpot in terms of potential returns. "Roof" money is "risk money," which I define as money you can afford to lose due to outside circumstances beyond your control.

There are several options to choose from that meet this strict definition of "risk money:"

- Individual stocks and ETFs (exchange traded funds)
- Mutual funds (both stock funds and bond funds)
- Variable annuities
- Commodities
- Options
- Managed futures
- Private equity
- Venture capital

The "roof" is traditionally where Wall Street, brokers and advisors love to put your money. In fact, I would guess that 95% of new clients who seek our advice have been told by their previous advisor to put 60%, 70%, 80%,

---

ROBERT'S RULE

When it comes to managing risk, it's important not to get bogged down in world events that you can't control or even influence. Instead, focus on what you CAN control, and that's how much to put into the roof of your fiscal dream home.

90% or even 100% of their life savings ALL into the roof. Wouldn't you agree that putting a large amount of money in the roof is terrible advice?

Yes, the roof is critical to have for potential growth, but it's exposed to all the outside elements that are beyond your control. Whether it's terrorist attacks, earthquakes, political mishaps, balance sheet fraud, high unemployment, or the ongoing European Union debt drama – realize you have no control over these events, but they certainly do affect your money that's invested in the roof.

When it comes to managing risk, it's important not to get bogged down in world events that you can't control or even influence. Instead, focus on what you CAN control, and that's how much to put into the roof of your fiscal dream home.

WHAT WOULD A PRUDENT INVESTOR DO?

I've found that one rule of thumb to limiting risk, in particular, has served investors well for over 100 years: the
"prudent investor rule." This rule states that a prudent
investor would limit their exposure to investments that
are risky, or as I call it "risk money."

Basically the prudent investor rule says you should
take 100 minus your age, and the remainder is the
MAXIMUM a prudent person would have in what I
consider the "roof."

So, if you're 62 years, old the max you should have in
the roof is 38% (100 – 62 = 38%). (Note: Knowing that we
are in the middle of a secular bear market, as explained
in an earlier chapter, it may be wise to trim your exposure
even further.)

INSULATING YOUR DREAM HOME

The roof of your fiscal dream home is only as good as
the walls that it's anchored to. And like the walls in
any well-built home, you need good insulation to keep
energy costs down. The walls of your fiscal dream home
are no different.

The walls are unique because they do not offer the
safe money feature of the foundation; nor do they offer
the risks of the roof. The walls provide stable cash flow,
inflation protection and insulation from market volatility.
The walls are made up of investments that must meet
three critical criteria:

- Little or no market correlation
- Stable cash flow
- Inflation protection (in a low-interest rate environment)

Because the definition of "wall" investments is so strict, only a few pass the "smell test" in the current market environment:

- Opportunistic real estate (not mutual funds or stocks)
- Secured floating income investments
- Natural resource exploration investments (NREs)

WHAT ARE THE PROS, CONS AND STRINGS ATTACHED?

One of the most critical things you need to understand about investing is that there is no such thing as a perfect investment. Every investment has a pro, a con, and always a string attached. Most advisors, brokers and bankers will tell you all the pros and maybe some of the cons, but rarely do they disclose the strings attached.

The investment vehicles that comprise your fiscal dream home are not exempt from this. They all have pros, cons and strings attached. Only when you understand all the benefits and drawbacks will you be able to make an educated decision before you sign on the dotted line.

As you move from the foundation to the roof, you move from safety to risk. But you expect a reward for that risk-taking don't you? Generally speaking, the lowest returns will come from the foundation, because they are at the lowest possible risk. The walls are positioned to offer middle-of-the-road returns because they are riskier than the foundation. The roof is where we look for the sizzle – the highest potential return, which obviously involves the highest risk.

When was the last time you dug up the foundation of your house? Hopefully you never have. Same goes for your fiscal dream home. The foundation is your longest term money, which IS the string attached. In the foundation, you trade access to the money to receive principal protection (which is another reason we don't want everything in the foundation).

The walls are intermediate-term – generally an anticipated holding period of five to seven years, but of course some wall investments are illiquid (and are typically only accessible by high-income earners and accredited investors). And the roof is by far the most liquid (and consequently the most uncertain), because you can always take the roof shingles off and put new ones on.

Here's the bottom line: The investments that may comprise your fiscal dream home may have differing levels and types of risks (cons), and it's important to understand that not one type of investment is perfect (like owning just mutual funds), but creating a balanced or harmonious strategy using many differing investments is what the ultra-wealthy and Yale do best. This is what has allowed them to earn higher than average returns with overall lower risk (see previous performance chart). This is what your fiscal dream home should seek to achieve as well.

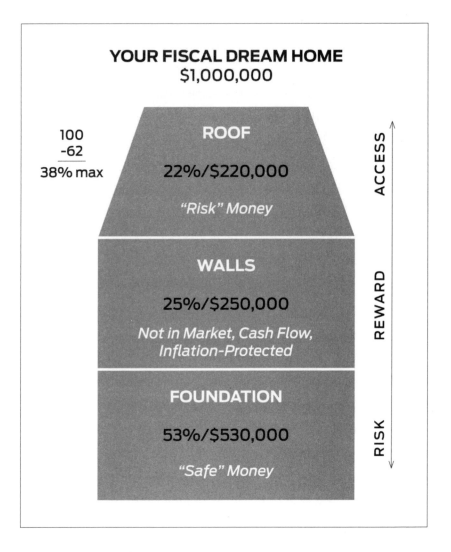

CONSTRUCTION BEGINS

If you were building your dream home, you would have a hand in picking out the faucets, tile, carpet, paint and so on. In other words, it's tailored to you – that's the benefit of building from scratch, from the foundation up – it fits you (and only you) perfectly! Your fiscal dream home is no different. It should be tailored to fit you exactly – your concerns, goals, tax sensitivity and income needs.

To provide a hypothetical example, let's assume you're 62 years old and married. You have amassed $1 million in retirement savings. You want lower risk and to be certain not to run out of money in retirement. Your allocations to the roof, walls and foundation may look something like the illustration at left.

ARE YOU READY TO RESCUE YOUR RETIREMENT?

In this book you've discovered how U.S. and global debt will affect your retirement, and you've learned tax strategies to keep more in your pocket.

You found out about the biggest threats to your wealth (inflation, RDCA and the next big bubble), and the investment secrets of the ultra-wealthy – the fiscal dream home.

You've learned behind-the-scenes techniques and secrets of the "smart money" crowd.

That's a lot of new information for anyone to absorb. Remember what I said about knowledge:

Knowledge is not power. Knowledge is potential power. It's what you do with the knowledge that gives you real power.

Vertical diversification may be the solution for putting sanity back into your investment strategy and helping you control risk while taking advantage of the investment strategies of the ultra-wealthy. But first you will need to find the right advice-giver (financial architect, if I may) to help you build your financial dream home.

The good news is that this is the easy part, because I'm about to hand over the tools necessary to help you find him/her. The hard part is actually coming to grips with the fact that you need the help – and ultimately deciding to rescue your retirement.

If you're ready to rescue your retirement from bad advice, simply turn the page.

Chapter 5

HOW TO HUNT FOR AND FIND THE RIGHT ADVICE-GIVER

"Being stuck is a position few of us like. We want something new but cannot let go of the old – old ideas, beliefs, habits, even thoughts. We are out of contact with our own genius. Sometimes we know we are stuck; sometimes we don't. In both cases we have to DO something."

– Rush Limbaugh

Man, I am impressed. Seriously, I am. Not only did you carefully read through the "meat" of this book, but also you're showing the necessary courage to free your retirement from captivity and unleash its full potential.

Now it's time to go on a hunt. A hunt for the right advice-giver.

I know what you may be thinking..."I've been with my advisor for years and I like him, he's a nice guy..."

Understand this, it's not about your advisor or money manager and hurting their feelings. It's all about you and your family. Take comfort that this is simply a business decision, it's nothing personal. That's right, it's simply a business decision to do what's right for you.

Here's a great quote from a legendary four-star general:

> *"The U.S. has been more hurt by the inability to make a decision than the decisions that have been made."*
>
> – *Colin Powell*

This chapter is designed to help you do just that: make an informed decision to find the right advice-giver, no matter where you live, in the United States or abroad.

AMATEUR HOUR IS OVER

If you've learned anything from this book, it's that amateur hour is over in the financial world.

I'm sure you would agree that a lot has changed in the financial world over the last several years. Consider this from a Sept. 2008 study cited in *The Wall Street Journal:*

> *"81% of investors with $1 million or more in invest-able assets plan to take money away from their current advisor. The irritation is especially high at the "brand" firms – large brokerages and banks. Fully 90% of their clients plan to take their money away from their current advisor."*

This illustrates three significant trends we are seeing consistently in our office, week in and week out:

- **Real, verified talent means something;** advisors will have to earn their keep now more than ever.
- **People who are serious about protecting their hard-earned wealth are demanding a second opinion,** and they are seeking advice from a recognized advisor with national media exposure.
- **People are tired of the old and failed buy/hold/ pray strategy.** They've lost faith in "the system;" they feel the game is rigged. They demand innovative approaches to wealth management that solve their unique problems.

You may be in the same situation as those cited in the study. In other words, you may have serious doubts about the decisions you've made and the choice of who you trust for retirement wealth advice.

The financial advisor who helped you get to this stage of your financial life may not be the right one to help you achieve your retirement dreams. Getting a second opinion and hiring the right advice-giver may be no easy task, but here are eight sure-fire steps to find the person who's right for you.

Step 1
DON'T GO IT ALONE

The rules of the retirement planning game are changing rapidly today. You need trusted guides who focus on solving these types of financial and legal problems. These trusted guides won't be found in the form of your favorite bank teller, nor at the local coffee shop, beauty salon or golf course.

The greatest protection available can be found by hiring the right wealth advisor who works with a specialized team of tax advisors, estate planning attorneys and money managers. A true advisor will help you manage the risks outlined in this book and surround himself/herself with a team of subject matter experts.

Step 2
IF IT SOUNDS TOO GOOD TO BE TRUE, IT PROBABLY IS

It's a common and scary trend today to hear retirees who have made poor decisions based on "buying into great opportunities." For instance, if a financial salesperson tells you about an 8% CD when you know darn well the bank down the road is paying 1.5% on CDs, guess what? That's a red flag – a giant, waving red flag.

When you hear something that sounds good and you want to believe it, ask the person this simple question: "What are the strings attached?" If they say "no strings," then you need to turn and run.

> ## ROBERT'S RULE
> ....
> When you hear something that sounds good and you want to believe it, ask the person this simple question: "What are the strings attached?" If they say "no strings," then you need to turn and run.

There are a lot of great financial products with attractive features, but even the great opportunities come with "rules" (aka "strings attached"). You need to know what they are and if they are acceptable to you and in line with your planning goals. Always use and trust your own good judgment and common sense.

Step 3
BEWARE OF "FREE"

Marketers use bait-and switch techniques on retirees constantly. Let me outline a few that we are very wary of.

First, let's dissect the free lunch or dinner seminar offer. Obviously, when you get an invitation saying, "Hey I'll buy you dinner," your good old common sense should kick in and say, "I need to be cautious here because this person may do something to get my money or sell me something." Red flag. I'm certainly not saying you shouldn't go to seminars to learn. We do educational events, but we invite people to come and learn from a nationally recognized financial educator or author.

Second, be careful of banks and credit unions that "refer" you to their in-house financial advisor. In reality, these people are financial salesmen. They often sell every bank customer the same expensive products – mutual funds and variable annuities. Again, "free" here ends up costing you money.

Step 4
WATCH OUT FOR LEGAL ADVICE FROM NON-LAWYERS

I know the value of integrating trust documentation and specific financial products. However, be very cautious when the purchase of a financial product also entitles you to free legal documents to support the plan. This is where you can be pennywise and fortune-foolish.

Our team approach at my wealth management firm is designed for collaboration among like-minded professionals focused on meeting the goals and objectives of our clients. No one professional can wear all of these hats and be good at all of these jobs.

A key defense from making a poor financial decision is to realize legal documents cost money; and a packaged offer with legal documentation included (based on the purchase of a product) should be a giant red flag.

Step 5
BEWARE OF ONLINE "RESOURCES"

Information online should be viewed with a very skeptical eye. Today it is not uncommon for retirees to jump online to do "research." The critical question is, are you getting information from a credible source? This can be very difficult to decipher online. Information overload is

> **Today it is not uncommon for retirees to jump online to do "research." The critical question is, are you getting information from a credible source? This can be very difficult to decipher online.**

another problem. If you enter the keywords "retirement advice" on Google, you'll come up with about 117 million search results. The problem is, before you finished looking at 117 million online "resources," you'd be more confused than ever and miss out on enjoying your retirement!

Yes, you need to do research, but on the right thing – finding the right help. Focus your due diligence on finding the right planning team to assist you.

Step 6
DEMAND PROOF

There's nothing worse than getting sold a bad idea. Slick talk can be very persuasive, but it may prove finan-cially disastrous. When seeking professional advice, I recommend that you assess just how accomplished your potential advice-giver really is. How that person answers the following questions should give you a good idea of their qualifications and passion for their work.

Are you a frequent contributor to the national financial media?

The top financial media outlets are looking for real experts, because they want their viewers and readers to get credible and accurate information. Both you and the national financial media need someone who doesn't just talk a good game, but someone who really knows his or her stuff. Not everyone appearing on CNBC, CNN, or FOX Business is a licensed advisor. In fact, many of these talking heads are spewing investment advice with no real background or credentials. These folks are there purely for entertainment value, not experienced wealth advice. Check out their background history via SEC/FINRA before acting on their hot tips!

Are you an author on this subject?

Professionals who take time to write have a passion for what they do. They've taken time to spell out their planning methods and beliefs. It's not easy writing a book or research report, so they are dedicated and serious about their profession and proud of what they do. Plus, you'll be able to obtain their book or report, read it and even get a second opinion about their message.

Do you invest in your professional knowledge?

This question is a great way to gauge the prospective advisor's commitment to staying current on new laws, tax code changes and cutting-edge ideas to help preserve and create wealth.

If you have a large IRA, you may be best served by an advisor that has trained with Ed Slott, a recognized CPA in the area of IRA planning. Likewise, an estate planning attorney who invests $20,000 a year to belong to an elite advisor coaching group is certainly educated on the latest and most effective estate planning strategies available to keep their clients' wealth "in the family" and away from the government.

Which professionals refer business to you?

It's common to ask for references, but I believe this is a loaded proposition because fully licensed advisors are restricted from providing testimonials. Furthermore, it wouldn't be too hard to find three or four people who like an advisor or lawyer and would give them a good

> **A number of high-level attorneys and tax advisors refer to us because they know we help their clients sleep well at night, especially during uncertain and chaotic times.**

reference. Our question is much different. A number of high-level attorneys and tax advisors refer to us because they know we help their clients sleep well at night, especially during uncertain and chaotic times. That certainly means more than just having a friend or client say nice things about us. The professional referral source has zero incentive to give false praise. To them it's all about how well we get the job done. This is a much more credible source of information to assess just how good an advisor or lawyer is at their craft.

Again, truly effective planning advice comes from well-organized teams of professionals, which is logical since no one person can be good at all things.

Step 7
BEWARE OF THE "COOKIE-CUTTER" FINANCIAL PLAN

Cookie cutters are for making cookies, not retirement plans. I think one of the largest problems and hidden truths about financial advisors is that many don't create customized plans to your unique goals and concerns. These financial salespeople use cookie-cutter plans wrapped carefully within clever sales and marketing pitches, disguised with the intent of making you believe their plan was made just for you.

Avoid strip malls for financial advice! I believe if you're going to a strip mall for financial advice you're probably getting strip mall quality advice.

I've had the privilege of reviewing hundreds of financial plans from some of the biggest and best advertised brokerage and mutual fund houses, and too often they are the same plans peddled over and over without regard to the individual's goals, concerns and problems. There's a real difference between investing and planning, and what you need at this stage of life is a plan as unique as your fingerprint.

To help make sure you don't end up with a cookie-cutter plan, be sure to ask some tough questions. Here's a short list to help:

- How does my plan differ from your other clients' plans?
- Do you rely on others to make buy/sell decisions on my investments?
- Has your parent company ever been sued for selling cookie-cutter plans?
- Do you have special selling agreements with outside investment companies that offer you bigger payouts for using their products?
- Is my plan unique to me? If so, how?

Step 8
BE SMART AND TRUST YOUR FEELINGS

Much is revealed when you meet face to face. See how you feel. When you walk through the door, you need to be treated as if you are a member of that practice's family. If you feel comfortable and more secure about your future after talking to them, then you may be in the right place.

Chapter 6
BEYOND THE BOOK

Kaizen: Japanese for continuous improvement or change for the better.

As of the time of writing this book, the strategies I've outlined are cutting-edge, but we all know that things change over time and innovation is a never-ending process.

Those of you who have been successful in life and business know that you can't stay at the top of your industry if you rest on your laurels.

I also know that to safely keep your retirement from being held hostage, you'll need to stay on top of events that can negatively affect your retirement. To make this easy and convenient for you, I've created a website, **www. RetirementHeldHostage.com,** to help you keep up with all the latest tips and strategies as well as access special reports and important information I uncover.

Be sure to visit **www.RetirementHeldHostage.com** to sign up for my free weekly report, "The Rob Report," our e-newsletter chock-full of great information and resources.

I welcome your correspondence and eagerly look forward to hearing your success stories.

I can be reached at:

Robert Russell

(800) 932-9418

TalkToRob@RetirementHeldHostage.com

Here's to rescuing your retirement from bad advice!

ACKNOWLEDGEMENTS

They say it takes an entire village to raise a child. While that may be correct, I can assure you that it takes an entire village to write a book.

Many people were instrumental during my two-year journey to complete this book. I've been so fortunate and blessed to be surrounded by some of the most talented and giving people in the world. Thanks for being there for me, encouraging me, sharing ideas and feedback, and putting up with me during the stressful times.

I would like to thank:

My Lord, who makes all things (including this book) possible. Thank you for inspiring me to help others and blessing me with my gifts. I hope I honor you with them.

Michelle, the smartest person I know, my wife and friend, for always believing in me and my crazy ideas. I know I keep you on your toes! You are my rock and biggest fan. Thanks for never giving up on me and reminding me of what's really important in life. I love you and am so proud of you.

Preston and Reagan, my little blessings. You never cease to amaze me. I don't know what I did to deserve the two of you, but I give thanks every day that I have the awesome responsibility of being your father. You are going to change the world in ways others only dream about, and I can't wait to witness it.

Dad, for believing in me and never giving up. You helped me go to college and provided sage wisdom along the way. You've been there all along, picking me up during tough times and helping me celebrate the good times. Thanks for teaching me so much and for giving me the room I needed to spread my wings.

Mom and Sonny, for the life lessons that helped form the person I am today. While I didn't understand the lessons at the time, I deeply value you for instilling my die-hard work ethic and competitive streak, and understanding the importance of family.

Cathy, for teaching me to stand up for what I believe in and giving me the strong backbone I needed. This has served me well as an adult, particularly during debates on FOX and CNBC!

Curv, the most positive person I've ever met – you're like a brother to me. I have enjoyed watching you blossom into an incredible wealth advisor and am proud to have played a tiny part it in. Thanks for helping me be more patient, enjoy every breath I take, and for challenging me. I'm so lucky to be alongside you.

Mike and Linda, for letting me have the honor of marrying your incredible daughter. I'm so thankful to have you in my life and have enjoyed our times together down on the farm.

Chief, my best friend, for your unswerving friendship. You always listen carefully and provide incredibly sage advice. You are wise beyond your years.

Faye Richardson (editor in chief), **Roberto Secades** (book cover designer) and **Alison Morse** (publisher), for making my dream come true by turning my "finger painting" into a "masterpiece." All of you are at the top of your respective fields and I couldn't be more thankful to have had the opportunity to work with you.

Pastor Jason, for your friendship, but more importantly for constantly challenging me. I've gained so much insight from you and loved our time together serving in Honduras. You are one of the rare breeds of people who make others feel like better people just by being in your presence.

Randy, for teaching me so much about leadership. You are a gifted mentor. God puts people in our life not by accident, and I'm thankful that I got to learn from you before running my company. I'm the CEO I am today because of you.

My team, the brightest, most dedicated people I've ever met. You are more than my employees; you are my partners. Oftentimes I get all the credit and publicity for my achievements, but really it's all of you who make me and our company so successful in helping secure our clients' retirement.

APPENDIX

[1]Source: www.CCH.com

[2]Each investment vehicle mentioned has varied levels of risks and liquidity, and potential investors should evaluate the differing fees, charges and expenses before making investment decisions. Principal protection of bank savings accounts and CDs are backed by FDIC. Fixed annuities and life insurance are backed by life insurance companies, and in addition, some states provide additional backing by state insurance guaranty associations. Some annuities contain charges for optional extra benefits such as income and death benefit riders. When purchasing life insurance, evaluate several different companies, their expenses and ratings. Annuities, CDs and life insurance should be considered mid- to long-term time commitments and may be subject to liquidation charges if surrendered early.

[3]Source: AARP July 2010

[4]Source: The City UK Financial Report 2011

[5]There are many alternative strategies that provide a good yield and have little or no correlation to interest rates or bond markets. Carefully laid out in a later chapter are some examples such as floating income investments, REITs, MLPs, etc.

[6]Source: Yale Endowment Fiscal Year 2011 and Harvard Managemet Company 12/2011

INDEX